TOP FUEL DRAGSTERS

Robert Genat

MBI Publishing Company

Dedication
To Don Garlits: The greatest Top Fuel racer of all time.

First published in 2002 by MBI Publishing Company, 380 Jackson Street, Suite 200, St. Paul, MN 55101-3885 USA

MBI Publishing Company books are also available at discounts in bulk quantity for industrial or sales-promotional use. For details write to Special Sales Manager at Motorbooks International Wholesalers & Distributors, 380 Jackson Street, Suite 200, St. Paul, MN 55101-3885 USA

Library of Congress Cataloging-in-Publication Data Available

ISBN 0-7603-1057-2

Edited by Amy Glaser

Designed by LeAnn Kuhlmann

On the front cover: Drag racing legend Shirley Muldowney lights up the tires prior to another run in Top Fuel. Muldowney was the first woman to be licensed to drive a Top Fuel dragster. Since 1973, she's been one of the fiercest competitors in Top Fuel. She has won 3 NHRA championships and 18 NHRA National events. After four decades of drag racing, Muldowney remains the single most accomplished woman competing in professional motorsports.

On the frontispiece: There can only be one Number One in the history of Top Fuel drag racing—"Big Daddy" Don Garlits. This is the upswept tail section on Garlits' Swamp Rat VI.

On the title page: Flames shoot six-feet high as two Top Fuel dragsters hit the throttle at the starting line. A small advantage in reaction time here can mean a big difference at the top end.

On the back cover: Because of the beauty of the front engine dragster, the mid-1960s has been called the Golden Age of Top Fuel. These four dragsters from that era were all built by the legendary car builder, Kent Fuller.

On the table of contents page: The burnout is the smoky prelude to a Top Fuel race. It's part of the ritual that is performed to make sure the car is prepared for the 4.5 second race at 330 miles per hour.

About the Author: Author Robert Genat has written more than 18 books for MBI Publishing Company. He is a highly skilled photographer and owns and operates Zone Five Photo. Robert and his wife, Robin, live in Encinitas, California.

Printed in China

Contents

Acknowledgments

I've got the greatest job on earth! Where can you get a gig like this that allows you to sit down and talk about racing with the legendary drivers of Top Fuel? Or stand by the side of the track as a modern Top Fueler rockets off the starting line on its way to a 300-mile-per-hour pass? Thanks to the following people who made my Top Fuel journey more fun than anyone should have: To "Big Daddy" Don Garlits and his staff at his Museum of Drag Racing for allowing me to remove cars from their permanent display so I could photograph them. Thanks go out to Greg Sharp and Steve Gibbs of the NHRA museum for all their help in allowing me to photograph the museum's cars and providing me with contacts within the sport. Thanks to the following Top Fuel greats who were kind enough to allow me to interview them: "TV" Tommy Ivo, Joaquin Arnett, Don "The Snake" Prudhomme, Tony Nancy, Shirley Muldowney, "Gentleman" Joe Schubeck, Joe Amato, Ed "The Ace" McCulloch, Bud Barnes, Bob Gladstone, Mike Kuhl, Carl Olson, Tommy "The Watchdog" Allen, Gary Scelzi, and Larry Dixon. Thanks to Bill Pitts for all the help, historical photos, and for keeping the flame alive by his restoration of the *Magicar*. Thanks to Jack Beckman and the staff at Frank Hawley's Drag Racing School for the ride of a lifetime. Thanks to the media relations departments at the NHRA and IHRA for their assistance, and to Chad Willis of Winston for all his help. Thanks to Carole Swartz and Lee Elder of Goodyear tires. A special thanks must go out to my good friend Joe Veraldi—in addition to helping me at photo shoots, he provided me with moral support at Frank Hawley's Drag Racing School. Thanks to my friend Don Cox for his exceptionally rare color historical photos, and thanks to Ron Lewis, Jere Alhadeff, and Larry Davis for their excellent historical photos.

Introduction

Top Fuel dragsters ferociously attack every one of the body's senses: sight, sound, and smell are all assaulted to the max. The white hot flames and billowing tire smoke are only a prelude to the high-speed quarter-mile show. While these cars are accelerating, the human eye can barely track their progress down the strip, much less see the changes that are happening to the car during the run. The apocalyptic sound of the 8,000-horsepower engine is like the devil's own brand of primeval thunder. Nitro, with its acrid smell, makes your eyes water and burns your lungs, but the hardcore fans love it. There's nothing on earth like Top Fuel dragsters.

Top Fuel dragsters are the fastest accelerating racecars in the world. A Top Fuel dragster reaches 100 miles per hour in less than 0.8 second, 200 miles per hour in 2.8 seconds, and 330 miles per hour in 4.5 seconds. They are also the fastest racecars to compete side by side in competition (100 miles an hour faster than CART or IRL open wheel racers). Their unique shape makes Top Fuel dragsters the most easily distinguished of any racecar. In addition, Top Fuel dragsters are the loudest racecars on the planet.

Top Fuel dragsters, also known as slingshots, diggers, or rails, have always had the advantage over other drag racing cars by virtue of their light weight. While coupes and roadsters were required to run with a body of some sort, dragsters were bare-bones racecars with a light frame, small seat, big engine, and a scant amount of bodywork. Power-to-weight ratios have always been high in Top Fuel dragsters. Today, a Top Fuel dragster has almost 3 horsepower for every pound of weight.

Reaching record-setting quarter-mile speeds in Top Fuel dragsters took a lot of innovation and hard work. This work was done by ordinary guys who were willing to try something new in the quest for more power. Unlike Formula One, in drag racing the best builders and tuners are not engineers with degrees. They are the same guys most of us rubbed shoulders with in auto shop class. Over the years, they didn't use any exotic calculations for building their cars—just seat-of-the-pants engineering. This commonsense style of building cars has been the hallmark in all classes of drag racing throughout the decades.

The birth of the Top Fuel dragster began with a simple set of frame rails and a fuel-burning flathead. During the 1960s, in what has been called the Golden Age of Top Fuel racing, the front engine dragster reached maximum refinement. This is also the era in which some of the most memorable races took place with legendary drivers at the wheel. The biggest change occurred when Don Garlits started the rear engine revolution. Since then, there has been no turning back.

The mid-1960s has often been called the Golden Age of dragsters. At that time there were hundreds of competitive Top Fuel dragsters across the country. The biggest concentration was on the West Coast, where chassis builders like Kent Fuller were designing and building some of the fastest and most beautiful Top Fuel dragsters, like the *Magicar*, seen here belching nitro flames.

The Golden Age of Top Fuel Dragsters

H ot rodders have always looked for the easiest way to produce horsepower. In the late 1940s to early 1950s they started placing additives of all kinds into pump gas. At that time, pump gasoline lacked the octane to produce much horsepower. Early racers of all types of cars tinkered with the fuel. If it was a liquid that produced a flame, it was tested. Methyl alcohol was one of the early favorites. It burned clean and allowed a hot rodder to substantially boost the compression ratio, thereby increasing power. Racers soon found that lacquer thinner, toluene, and other magical additives didn't do that much for power. Nitromethane became the preferred liquid medium of power.

In the mid-1950s, dragsters were stripped down roadsters. Here the blue Renck Electric dragster takes on a red roadster. Although both cars are equipped with roll bars, they certainly wouldn't have done the driver much good, since both drivers' heads extend beyond the height of the bars. The driver of the red roadster must feel confident that his car won't roll over, because he has decided not to wear a helmet. ©Don Cox

Nitromethane became the preferred liquid medium of power. Nitromethane produces power because one of the components of the compound is oxygen. Because nitro brings its own oxygen to the party, air-fuel ratios of as high as one-to-one can be run. Joaquin Arnett was one of the early users of nitromethane. Prior to building dragsters, he ran a roadster at the drags. "When I'd run stock-bodied on gas, it would run 90 to 100 miles per hour," recalls Arnett. "Nitro would boost the speed to 115 or 118." Arnett claimed to run nothing but a fifty–fifty mixture because it was the easiest to mix consistently. This small addition to the fuel added 20 percent to his car's horsepower with no other modifications.

Drag racing events were popping up all over the country in the mid-1950s. In 1954, an Ohio-based club called the Cam Jammers organized drag races. The races began on an abandoned road, and were later held at the airport in Akron, Ohio. The youthful future drag racing great, Joe Schubeck, attended these races. "I got the bug to build a dragster right out of the chute," recalls Schubeck. He worked with a friend to build a dragster from a set of Model T rails. It was powered by a 296-ci flathead with three Stromberg carbs. "We went to straight nitromethane in it," boasts Schubeck. At the time, Schubeck was a senior in high school. "The funny thing about that car was that it was a school project, but the school never knew about it." Many of the high-school machine shop and auto mechanics students all contributed to the sponsorship of Joe's racecar. "I'd bring it behind the school and fire it up on nitromethane; it was quite a distraction and attention getter."

Schubeck's girlfriend's father used nitromethane in his paint and paint thinner business. He would sell it to Joe for 75 cents a gallon. "I thought, God, this guy's really screwing me. Gasoline was only 25 cents a gallon." In addition to the nitromethane,

Schubeck added a little benzene as an ignitor. "We called it 'shoe polish' because it had a sweet smell, like something right out of a shoe polish bottle," says Schubeck.

One of Schubeck's most memorable races with that car was against Walt Affron's appropriately named *Bologna Slicer.* Affron's dragster had a Ranger aircraft engine with a pusher-style propeller in the rear. The *Bologna Slicer* was slow off the line, but it had a good top end charge. "I remember lining up against that *Bologna Slicer* and I used to get him out of

Early dragsters often looked more like stretched sprint cars than dragsters. This is the Duncan-Losinski injected Hemi dragster at an early SCTA (Southern California Timing Association)-sponsored meet in Colton, California. ©*Don Cox*

Art Chrisman was a dry lakes racer who also raced at the drags. His Chrisman-Canon *Hustler* was one of the hottest dragsters in the country in 1959. In February, 1959, Chrisman ran the quarter-mile at 181.81 miles per hour and won the Smokers meet.

the chute," says Schubeck. "And right at the end, he'd come by on the two-lane road they used for the drag strip with that spinning propeller about 5 feet away from me at about 150 miles per hour. I was too young and crazy to realize how dangerous that was, but at the time I thought it was a great thrill."

Up through 1956, nitromethane was the accepted alternative fuel for drag racing, but it was a double-edged sword. Nitro created speeds beyond the technology of the rest of

the car and most of the tracks on which the cars ran. Braking systems on the cars in the 1950s were barely adequate to stop those running on gas, much less those running at higher speeds on nitro. For the 1957 season, the NHRA (National Hot Rod Association) took a bold step and banned the use of all fuels other than pump gasoline. A few of the independent drag strips also joined the ban. The NHRA was not the powerhouse sanctioning body it is today. It was only one of many

In 1959, Don Garlits was invited to the Smokers Fuel and Gas Championships that were held in Bakersfield, California. He brought out his *Swamp Rat I*, but was unsuccessful.

sanctioning bodies, most of which allowed exotic fuels in their program.

Drag racers who wanted to run nitro could compete at the many other tracks that allowed its use. The restriction to gasoline built an unusual fire under the competitors who had abandoned nitro. They went back to the drawing boards and worked on every aspect of their cars to make them faster. No longer able to lean on the comfortable crutch of liquid horsepower, they had to improve

chassis and engine technology if they wanted to go faster. This led to new lightweight chassis designs, advanced blower drives, and improved fuel injectors. In addition, many competitors built twin-engine cars.

Two years into the fuel ban, a landmark event took place in the history of Top Fuel racing—the 1959 March Meet. The March Meet was the first of several events sponsored by the Smokers Car Club of Bakersfield, California. It was held at Famoso drag strip, which

Don Garlits' *Swamp Rat I* was powered by a carbureted Chrysler Hemi engine. Shortly after attending the 1959 Smokers meet, Garlits added a GMC supercharger.

defense plan to have southern California blanketed with air strips, the entire place was paved. In 1959, and for several years to follow, this would be drag racing's equivalent of Woodstock, because the hard-core fans would make a pilgrimage to an event that wasn't advertised or heavily promoted.

Don Garlits had been invited out for the 1959 meet. Everyone on the West Coast was skeptical of the speeds and elapsed times he was running and wanted to see if he could run those times on "accurate" clocks. When Garlits arrived, people were amazed at the lack of sophistication in his car and equipment. His dragster was based on an old set of Chevy frame rails with a carbureted Chrysler Hemi engine. Garlits unloaded his car and promptly ran a respectable 9.00-second elapsed time at a speed of 172.41 miles per hour. On the evening prior to the Sunday eliminations, Garlits swapped engines, and hoped for more speed. Unfortunately, all he received for his hard work was anguish—his engine blew. In addition to the pain of a broken engine, rumors were circulating among the fans and racers that Garlits had sabotaged his own engine to avoid competing head-to-head with the California cars.

Art Chrisman won the 1959 Smokers meet in the Chrisman-Canon *Hustler*. Chrisman came to the meet as one of the favorites, having run a record-shattering 181 miles per hour one month before. Even back in 1959, money made horsepower, and Frank Canon was the one who financed Chrisman's car. Chrisman and his brother Lloyd constructed the car and built the engine. Their dragster featured a ladder frame constructed out of 2 1/2-inch-diameter chrome moly tubing. Up front was a 1937 Ford tubular axle with a transverse spring and friction shocks. The narrowed rear end was a 1941 Ford with a Halibrand quick-change and

was built on an old World War II airstrip and was named for the frontage road that bordered the old airfield. By today's standards, it was a dangerous place to race or watch a race. There were no bleachers for the fans, but thanks to the government's World War II

This simple red dragster was Don Prudhomme's first Top Fuel dragster. It was originally owned by Tommy Ivo and ran an injected Buick engine on gas. Shortly after obtaining it from Ivo, Prudhomme switched to a fuel-burning Chrysler.

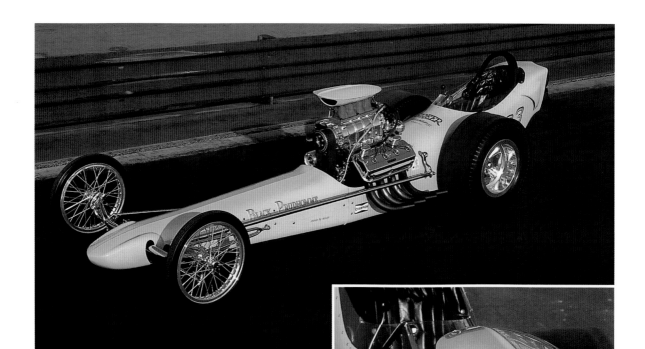

Because of Prudhomme's superb driving skills, he was hired to drive the *Greer-Black-Prudhomme* Top Fuel dragster. Between June 1962, and May 1963, this car won almost every race it entered. It could run the quarter in just under 7 seconds at a little over 190 miles per hour.

Lincoln brakes. The Chrysler Hemi engine featured a standard bore with a 1/2-inch additional stroke. On top was a GMC (General Motors Corporation) supercharger fed by Hilborn injectors.

The excitement of the 1959 Smoker's meet was exactly what drag racing and Top Fuel dragsters needed. Now, everyone wanted to see Top Fuel dragsters race. This race also confirmed that to be competitive in Top Fuel you needed a blower. Garlits became a convert and installed one on his car before he left California. He tried out the new combination at

Powering the *Greer-Black-Prudhomme* dragster was a Chrysler Hemi engine built by Keith Black. In the early 1960s, Black and Dave Zeuschel were the two best Top Fuel engine builders.

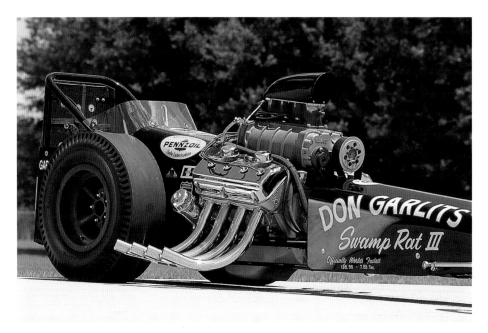

Don Garlits' *Swamp Rat III* was built in 1961 and raced through the 1962 season. Driven by Connie Swingle, its best time was 7.88 seconds at 198.96 miles per hour.

In 1964, the *Michigander* was built and tuned by Bob Gladstone and driven by Bud Barnes. It featured a Logghe chassis and fuel-burning Chrysler Hemi with "weed burner" headers. In June 1967 *The Michigander* ran an 8.07-second elapsed time at a speed of 197 miles per hour at Santa Pod Raceway, in England. Its best time in the United States was a 7.37-second elapsed time at a speed of 207 miles per hour.

Two Top Fuelers charge off the line in a cloud of smoke at Carlsbad Raceway in Carlsbad, California. The driving technique for a Top Fuel dragster in 1964 was to simply slide your left foot off the clutch while standing on the accelerator. ©*Bill Pitts*

Kingdon, California, where he won the race. On the way home to Florida, he stopped in Chandler, Arizona, and won again.

Unfazed by the success of the March Meet, the NHRA continued its ban of nitro, which it had instituted in 1957. Those who raced on anything other than gasoline simply didn't run at NHRA-sanctioned strips. Winning an NHRA national event only brought you a trophy and a few photos in *Hot Rod* magazine. Match racing and the big fuel events brought more money and prestige.

It was during this time that the front engine dragster evolved from a machine that looked like a modified sprint car into a purpose-built slingshot dragster. In the early 1960s, old passenger car frame rails were set aside in favor of custom-built chassis of chrome moly tubing. Wheelbases grew longer, and the cars were fitted with stylish bodywork. The Chrysler Hemi was the Top Fuel engine of choice, and every one of them was equipped with a blower. Nitro percentages ran from 50 to 100 percent.

"Gentleman" Joe Schubeck brought his *Lakewood Chassis* dragster out from Ohio for the 1965 March Meet. Schubeck qualified 36th in a 64-car field with an elapsed time of 7.95 seconds at a speed of 194.38 miles per hour. ©*Bill Pitts*

The Frantic Four—Weekly, Rivero, Fox, and Holding—entered this car at the 1965 March Meet, with "Stormin'" Norman Weekly at the wheel. It qualified 31st with a 7.93-second elapsed time. It was in the mid-1960s that the exhaust headers on dragsters went from the weed burner style to the zoomies that were aimed up and back toward the tires. ©*Bill Pitts*

"TV" Tommy Ivo was one of the best Top Fuel drivers of all time. His cars were expertly crafted and consistently fast. This is the car he entered in the 1965 March Meet, where he qualified 44th.
©Bill Pitts

One of the top drag racers of all time was "TV" Tommy Ivo. In the late 1950s, his gas-burning, twin-engine Buick dragster put him on the drag racing map. That car was followed by his four-engine dragster. Ivo couldn't resist the temptation of the speed and showmanship that Top Fuel dragsters gave the fans. "I went into partnership with Zeuschel when I first started running the fueler because I didn't trust myself—I didn't know anything about fuel motors," recalls Ivo. The partnership only lasted about six months, for two main reasons: Ivo liked to do all of his own work, and he didn't particularly like partners. "Everybody always thought I had a mechanic and that I'd fly in with my white gloves to see if it's clean, and say, 'OK let's run!' Then fly out again. It wasn't that way at all." Ivo was an accomplished mechanic, car builder, and driver.

Like all of Ivo's cars, his fueler was good-looking and fast. "I was the first one to run in the sevens," boasts Ivo. About two weeks later, Prudhomme broke into the 7-second range. "Then we raced each other at San Gabriel (on February, 24, 1963), and that was the first 7-second side-by-side run."

In the early 1960s, Ivo and Don Garlits did a lot of match racing across the country. Both had excellent Top Fuel cars, and both were outstanding drivers. At one match race, Ivo played one of his famous pranks on Garlits. Prior to the final run, he went over to Garlits' pit area and told him, "I burned a piston on the last run, so if I get out on ya, keep an eye on me so I don't get a face full of oil." This professional courtesy was intended to let Garlits know that Ivo's engine might blow up on the next run. Often, when an engine in a front engine dragster exploded, the driver got a face full of oil and couldn't see where he was going and might drift into the competitor's lane. In reality, Ivo's engine was just fine.

The *Vagabond* was originally built by Kent Fuller in 1962 for Jim Van Ronk and Roy Bumgardner. In this car on June 9, 1965, at the Excelsior Drag Strip in Sacramento, California, driver Gary Ormsby was the first to top 200 miles per hour (201.34).

His comments were part of an elaborate Ivo hoax. Prior to the run, unbeknownst to Garlits, Ivo had taken a can of STP and poured it down one of the header pipes on his car. The cars were push-started and when they reached the turn-around area, Ivo's car was billowing smoke. "He looked over and saw smoke coming out," recalls Ivo. "He must have said to himself, 'Well, Ivo's dead, I'll take it nice and easy.'" They both staged, and Ivo's car still had

The Sour Sisters' car was affectionately known as the "Shark Car" for obvious reasons. In the mid-1960s, many Top Fuel dragsters had stylish fairings at the rear of the body. Even though the engine says "Oldsmobile" on the valve cover, it's still a Chrysler Hemi. ©*Bill Pitts*

The Midwest may not have had as many Top Fuel competitors as the West Coast, but the ones they had were some of the best. This is the Logghe-built *Prussian* that was driven by Maynard Rupp. At the 1965 March Meet, it qualified 16th with an elapsed time of 7.79 seconds at 195.80 miles per hour. ©*Larry Davis*

Don Garlits broke with tradition when he debuted his red *Swamp Rat VI*. Soon, it was painted "Garlits' black" and tearing up the strips. This is the first of Garlits' *Swamp Rats* to run over 200 miles per hour.

smoke pouring out of the one cylinder. When the light turned green, Ivo was gone and left Garlits behind in a cloud of smoke.

Ivo and Garlits were also part of the U.S. Drag Racing Team that the NHRA sent to England in September 1964. The NHRA had eased its ban on nitro the year before and wanted to give the British the best show possible by bringing along two of the best nitro racers. Garlits brought along his *Swamp Rat*

VI, the car in which he won the U.S. Nationals. Tony Nancy brought his *Wedge II* gas dragster. Also attending were top A/FX racers Ronnie Sox and Dave Strickler. The Gas Coupes were represented by K.S. Pitman and George Montgomery.

On Saturday, September 19, the British fans got to see their first dose of real drag racing. The Brits had never seen anything like the American dragsters. "We had the thunder,"

At the 1965 March Meet, Don Prudhomme drove Roland Leong's *Hawaiian* dragster and was considered a favorite following their Winternationals Top Fuel win. Prudhomme qualified 20th with a pass of 7.83 seconds. Many feel that the *Hawaiian*, built by Kent Fuller, was the most beautiful dragster of the front engine dragster era. Prudhomme's top speed for this car in 1965 was 215.56 miles per hour. ©*Bill Pitts*

Conrad "Connie" Kalitta started out driving gas dragsters and eventually moved into Top Fuelers. When Ford Motor Company passed out its single overhead cam (SOHC) engines to selected racers, he was at the head of the line. On May 7, 1966, Kalitta ran 221.12 miles per hour in this car at Capitol City Raceway in Maryland.

This Top Fuel dragster is typical of mid-1960s California design and construction. It features a sleek, stylish body with a brilliant metal flake paint job highlighted by lots of chrome and polished magnesium. The trailer is a four-wheel flatbed with mag wheels. ©*Bill Pitts*

says Ivo proudly. Ivo, showing respect for Garlits' status in the sport, asked if Garlits minded if he made the first run. "I thought I was gonna have to fight Garlits for the first run," says Ivo. "Garlits was gung ho; he said, 'Go ahead and make the first run.' He wanted to see what the track was like." Ivo recalls Garlits working on his car as if it were the U.S. Nationals, whereas Ivo's first priority was having fun. "We had just come up with the zoomies (headers) at the time," says Ivo. "I took the zoomies off and put on the weed

burners, 'cause they were twice as long and made much more noise. The heck with racing! I wanted to show these limeys something that was worthwhile." The tracks they were running on were old Royal Air Force landing fields that were 2,400 feet wide and 2 to 4 miles long. They were also in terrible condition because they had been bombed and patched during the war. "They were the worst thing you could ever run on," recalls Ivo.

Ivo made the first pass and recorded an 8.40 elapsed time at a speed of 184 miles per

Prior to his untimely death in 1971, Pete Robinson was one of the most successful gas dragster racers, winning the 1961 U.S. Nationals in a Chevy-powered dragster. In 1966, he switched to the Ford Cammer engine and was the first to win a major NHRA meet with Ford's new powerhouse. Robinson also developed many of the specialized components used on the blown Cammer engines.

Front engine dragster drivers were required to peer around the massive supercharged Hemi engine to see the track. Engines often blew up, covering the driver with hot oil, water, and even worse, flames. Aluminized facemasks with breathers helped, but it was still a dangerous job.

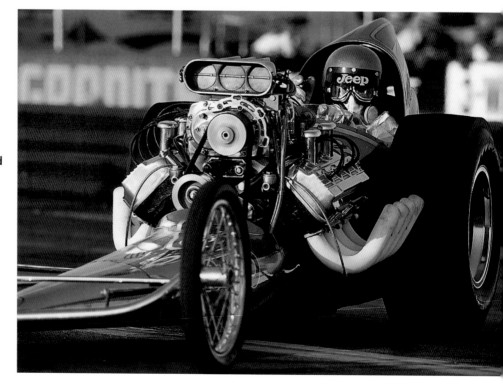

Don Garlits built the 200-inch wheelbase chassis for his *Swamp Rat 12C*, also known as the *Wynns Charger*. It was powered by a 500-ci Dodge Hemi and featured a stunning red-and-black paint scheme over a Tom Hanna body.

hour. In doing so he smoked the tires for the entire distance. The sound of nitro through the weed burners was something never before heard in England. The English fans also had never seen a car with so much power that it could spin the tires at 180 miles per hour. Garlits followed Ivo and ran 8.28 at 188 miles per hour. On that tour, Garlits set the British Land Speed Record at 197 miles per hour.

Powering the Top Fueler of the early 1960s was the Chrysler Hemi. It was a heavy engine, but it could take a lot of abuse in stock form. These engines were produced in several displacements between 1951 and 1959. The later

392-ci version was the drag racer's favorite. Many of the low-buck teams ran them stock, adding only a blower and injectors. The competitors with more money were able to afford custom-built engines that featured forged pistons and roller cams. Professionally built engines were used for consistency more than for additional power. One of these early Hemi engines produced well over 1,000 horsepower when nitro was used. These engines lasted a long time because the tires spun for the entire quarter, never hooking up and placing a load on the engine. The limiting factor to lower elapsed times and higher speeds in Top Fuel

In 1966, Mike Snively drove Roland Leong's *Hawaiian* at the March Meet, where he ran 207 miles per hour. In 1967, he would win the March Meet in this car. ©*Bill Pitts*

In 1966 Don Prudhomme towed his silver *Torque Master Special* into the March Meet. His simple flat-bed trailer had two wheels and the trunk of the Cadillac tow car was weighed down with tools and a few spare parts. This is a long way from the rigs used for today's Top Fuel dragsters. ©*Bill Pitts*

was not horsepower. The cars had more than they could use. It was the tires. Whenever an improved slick was introduced, elapsed times dropped and speeds increased.

Driving a front engine dragster was not a task for the faint-hearted. Being strapped in behind a fire-breathing, 1,000-horsepower engine filled with volatile liquids took a lot of guts. It also took a lot of courage to place your most precious God-given body parts on top of the differential and one foot on either side of the clutch. To see down the strip, the driver had to look around the blower. With zoomie headers, the noise from the exhaust was aimed back at the driver. "Those headers came right back by your ears," says Ivo. "I used to take old shop towels, tear 'em in half, and fold

'em over and put them inside my helmet, so it was as quiet as a mouse." Even with the noise, the ride was spectacular—especially at night. "You'd sit there, and there would be these two big pillars of flame standing outside the motor," recalls Ivo. "You hit it and the smoke goes up, and all the smoke would turn into a big orange cloud above you. It was great!"

The technique to driving one of these early fuelers was simple—sidestep the clutch and stand on the gas. The tires would instantly turn into white smoke that was driven into the sky by the zoomie headers. There was a small window between the blower and smoke where the driver could see ahead. Most drivers will tell you that the ride was pretty smooth. It wasn't until tire technology

improved that the car started to shake. As the speed increased, the smoke was blown rearward. At the top end, the driver could see the slicks growing in diameter as the speed increased. Often, as the cars went through the traps, the engine would blow oil out of the breathers into the driver's face. There's nothing like a face full of oil at 190 miles per hour!

Most drivers worked their way up from lower-class gas dragsters to a fuel burner. Tommy "The Watchdog" Allen successfully drove a Chevy-powered gas dragster for two years. "I'd made hundreds of passes down the quarter-mile in my little Chevy-powered dragster," recalls Allen. Because of his experience with the Chevy rail, he felt the transition to a fuel-burning dragster would be easy. "The first time I stepped on the pedal on the Chrysler, I just about passed out. I couldn't believe the difference!" In addition to being much louder than his gas-burning Chevy, the acceleration and resultant G-forces were increased. "The most difficult part is getting your mind to catch up with the acceleration. Anybody who hasn't driven a dragster has no clue at all." At first Allen thought he'd never be able to drive a Top Fuel car. Soon, he settled in and was the first to officially run over 210 miles per hour (211.76) in a Top Fueler.

One of the most fearsome cars to emerge from the front engine dragster era was the *Greer-Black-Prudhomme* dragster. It combined an expertly crafted chassis, a professionally built engine, and a world-class driver. The car was initially built by Kent Fuller for Ron Stuckey. Following a fatal accident involving

Tommy Ivo's 1966 Top Fuel dragster featured a swoopy rear body with a built-in horizontal wing. In 1965 and 1966, Top Fuel dragster chassis were all getting longer (150 to 175 inches). ©*Bill Pitts*

In 1969, Larry Dixon, driving the *Howard Cams Rattler*, was the Top Eliminator at the big race sponsored by *Hot Rod* magazine. Jerry Johansen built the 392-ci Chrysler that propelled this car to an elapsed time of 6.74 at a speed of 224 miles per hour.

Stuckey, it ended up at Fuller's shop, where Tommy Greer bought it. He had Keith Black build the engine, and they selected Don Prudhomme as the driver. Prudhomme had just won the 1962 March Meet and was the hottest young driver around. Starting in June 1962, and running through May 1963, the *Greer-Black-Prudhomme* car was almost unbeatable and won nearly every race it entered. The only big loss was at the 1963 March Meet, where Prudhomme was beaten by Art Malone, who went on to win the event.

The March Meet's popularity continued to grow in terms of the number of cars competing, as well as in attendance. In 1964, 32 dragsters were in the show and Connie Kalitta came out on top. In 1965, there was an astounding 64-car field. Joe Schubeck, now called "Gentleman Joe," had progressed well beyond his high-school

auto shop flathead fueler, and brought his *Lakewood Chassis* dragster from Ohio to qualify 36th. "I thought I'd died and gone to dragster heaven," exclaims Schubeck. "I remember there were cars fired up at the crack of dawn. Nitro fumes were everywhere from the time the sun came up until it was too dark to see."

For four days straight, this was the best Top Fuel show ever. As two cars were being push-started on the return road, two others were making the turn-around at the starting line, and two more were leaving the starting line. The smoke just never seemed to clear. Every big name in drag racing was at the meet. "I had the pan off and I was checking the bearings on my car. Oil was dripping in my face and I was loving every second," recalls Schubeck. "Then this guy slides underneath and says, 'Let me help.' I looked over and it was Mickey Thompson." Schubeck had never met Thompson before, but had read about his racing exploits. "It might as well have been St. Joseph or God! Then he starts helping me change the bearings and I'm thinking I really am in heaven. Here's Mickey Thompson laying on his back helping me change the bearings in my car. The people back home would never believe this." It was that kind of meet. Every future legend of the sport was there. At the end of the fourth day, Don Garlits came out as the winner of the 1965 Smokers meet. The 1966 show also fielded 64 cars, and Mike Sorokin drove *The Surfers* car to the win.

In 1967, the popularity of Top Fuel dragsters was challenged by Funny Cars. The March Meet was promoted as a Funny Car show and many of the big name Top Fuel drivers passed up the event. The NHRA had also reinstated the Top Fuel class a few years earlier and had expanded the number of national events. While the popularity of drag racing was growing, Top Fuel was beginning to take a back seat to Funny Cars, but the allure of speed still enticed new and old drivers to the Top Fuel class.

With the exception of his first fuel-burning roadster, drag racing legend Tony Nancy's race-cars ran on gas. "Prudhomme used to ask me all the time," recalls Nancy, "'What do you run that parts-wash stuff for? Put some horsepower in that motor and put some nitro in it.'" Nancy felt that the cost of the fuel was too high. At that time, he didn't think he knew enough about how to tune an engine running fuel. "I found out how much easier it was to tune with nitro than it was with gasoline. With gasoline, I had to make a lot of muscle with what was there. With nitro, you could run 92 or 97 percent, run

Technical inspection for the 1966 U.S. Nationals was held in an Indianapolis area shopping center parking lot. All of the cars expecting to compete were unloaded and queued up in one of the several long lines of racecars. Here, Connie Kalitta's Cammer-powered dragster awaits its turn with the inspectors. ©*Larry Davis*

60 degrees in the mag, and play with blower ratios." Nancy found that the motor responded well to each tuning technique.

Tony Nancy never did anything halfway. He always bought the best he could afford. Once he decided to go Top Fuel racing, he called Woody Gilmore to order a dragster chassis. "They were about halfway through with the car and I went down to the shop to see how they were doing." As Nancy walked into the shop, he saw three future legends of drag racing working on his car. "I looked and there's Paul Sutherland, John Buttera, and Woody Gilmore working on it. Tom Hanna built the body. I couldn't ask for a better bunch of guys." Chrysler sent Nancy a new late-model Hemi. "I talked to KB [Keith Black] about it. We were all impressed by the size of the combustion chamber." Black was the master of Top Fuel Hemi engines. "KB was willing to give me a little advice about what to do. He never really told you what to do. He'd say, 'Well, you might try this.' He made you work out your own problems."

Nancy was still concerned about running the new car on fuel and called his old friend Prudhomme. He told Nancy not to worry; he would help him through the process. Prudhomme suggested running at San Fernando drag strip during the week and agreed to come along. Prudhomme also gave Nancy his tune-up to get him started. "He gave me his combination at San Fernando and we ran the car. The car ran so well that we came back on Sunday and broke the strip record for e.t. and speed." The following week Nancy took the car to Long Beach and raced competitively. "I was hooked—I became a fuel junkie." Nancy vowed to never put anything but nitro in a racecar again. "I didn't give a damn if there wasn't a spectator in the stands and we could just make pass after pass down there. I just enjoyed it." With every pass Nancy learned more about running a fuel car and was able to dial it in even better. Nancy confesses that he couldn't have done it without his old friend Don Prudhomme. "I gotta thank Don Prudhomme for the help that he gave me on it." One of Nancy's biggest wins was at the 1970 March Meet.

The death knell for the front engine dragster era officially rang on March 8, 1970, with a sudden explosion on the starting line at Lions Drag Strip. Don Garlits was lined up against Richard Tharp in the Creitz-Donovan dragster. When the light went green, Garlits stepped on the pedal and his *Swamp Rat XIII* was instantly blown in two. The transmission he was using exploded and the parts penetrated the quarter-inch steel case and safety blanket. Garlits' first thought was that he had blown the clutch in the timing lights, and he was sure he was going to be killed while tumbling at high speed. When the roll cage came to a stop, Garlits realized he was only a short distance from the starting line. He then saw the blood and felt extreme pain in his right foot. In addition to the end of his right foot being cut off, Garlits also sustained a broken left leg and two bones in his left foot were broken. This event prompted Garlits to never race a front engine dragster again.

Against the advice of others, Garlits and his friend, Connie Swingle, began construction on a new rear engine dragster. It would be named *Swamp Rat XIV*, it would be painted black, and it would make history.

Opposite: **Nitromethane creates a lot of heat as it burns. As Carl Olson pulls Mike Kuhl's dragster to the line, the headers are already glowing orange from the heat of combustion.**

In 1991, Top Fuel driver Dick LaHaie has a lot going on as he clears the traps at 290 miles per hour. First and foremost, the engine is in the process of self-destructing. He has popped the chute to help slow the car. The aerodynamic forces generated by the speed have flexed almost every body panel on the front of the car. Finally, at these speeds, the slicks distort as they come in contact with the track. ©Ron Lewis

The Rear Engine Era

D on Garlits' accident at Lions Drag Strip on March 8, 1970, would become a landmark date in drag racing history. He had suffered several fiery engine explosions in his career, but none was as devastating as the one in Long Beach that sliced his car in two and amputated half of his right foot. Garlits was lucky. Others had been killed driving front engine dragsters. Every painful step he took on his ravaged right foot convinced him that the driver should sit in front of the engine instead of behind it.

The momentum of the front engine dragster stopped abruptly in 1971 when Don Garlits rolled his revolutionary rear engine dragster,

Swamp Rat XIV, off the trailer at Pomona and won the NHRA Winternationals. Garlits' rear engine car would become the model for all future Top Fuel dragsters. The rear engine dragster would dominate the class, provide a much safer racing environment for the driver, and ultimately revolutionize Top Fuel racing. "A lot of people had a laugh," recalls Don Garlits.

"They didn't think rear engine cars were ever going to amount to anything." Although the front engine dragster was extremely dangerous, it was the accepted standard for 10 years and had been developed into a fast racing machine that produced a great show for race fans.

Garlits' first rear engine car had a few teething problems. On his first runs he had

With this car in 1971, Don Garlits forever changed the face of Top Fuel drag racing. Rear engine dragsters proved to be better balanced racecars, and they provided the drivers with a larger margin of safety. ©*Ron Lewis*

Carl Olson, winner of the 1972 NHRA Winternationals, pulls to the line in the Kuhl & Olson Top Fuel dragster. Olson, who had previously driven front engine dragsters, found the rear engine dragster easier to drive. The addition of the rear wing instantly cut 1/10 of a second from the car's elapsed time.
©Jere Alhadeff

problems with directional stability. Garlits' friend, sometime-driver, and chassis welder Connie Swingle, suggested slowing down the steering ratio. This was the key to improved handling. Tests at the Sunshine Dragstrip in St. Petersburg, Florida, in December 1970 gave Garlits the confidence to believe that he had built another winner. Garlits packed up *Swamp Rat XIV* and headed West for the first races of the 1971 season. Garlits lost the first two races he entered, the AHRA (American Hot Rod Association) Grand American race at Lions and the Orange County International Raceway All-Pro Series race. The third race, the NHRA Winternationals, would be the charm. From that day on, Garlits dominated the sport in his new dragster. "By the time I got one," says Prudhomme, "Garlits had already put the wing on the back. The whole sport had changed. I mean everyone was running crazy. You gotta build a rear engine car! But nobody knew anything about it and Garlits was real secretive about what he had. It was a mad panic to catch up with him."

Following Garlits' 1971 Winternationals win, he took to the tracks of America and convinced everyone that his rear engine car was the way of the future by winning 80 percent of the races he entered. He also became the AHRA's 1971 Top Fuel champ. While Garlits' design was initially driven by safety, he unknowingly developed a much better race-car, as the rear engine design inherently offered better balance. By 1973, all of the old front engine dragster chassis were hanging from the rafters and collecting dust. A Top

Two restoration experts at Don Garlits' Museum of Drag Racing fit the wing to this recently restored monocoque rear engine dragster, built by chassis builder John Buttera, with the help of Louie Techenoff and Nye Frank. This was one of many rear engine dragster experiments in the early 1970s. It was campaigned for a short time by Barry Setzer, but was unsuccessful due to the rigidity of the monocoque chassis.

Fuel racer now had to run a rear engine dragster to be competitive. With the rear engine, speeds increased and elapsed times dropped. Fans who had been lured away by Funny Cars were coming back to watch the Top Fuel races because of the increased speed and new cars.

For the drivers, it was an easy switch to the rear engine configuration. They had the comfort of knowing that if an engine blew, they would not be covered in water, hot oil, engine parts, or fire. Instead of looking around an engine and blower to see the track, they now had clear visibility of the strip and both front wheels. Also, with the engine in the rear, the drivers no longer had the booming stereo effect of the zoomie headers roaring in their ears. The driver could hear what was going on with the engine and not just the exhaust note. The improved balance of the racecar made it much easier to drive because the car's front wheels were in contact with the racetrack more than they had been with the front engine car. For most Top Fuel drivers, this new configuration created a level of comfort never before felt in a racecar.

Another major development that would change the future of drag racing also happened in 1971—the aluminum Hemi block. Up until then, Top Fuel competitors were running either the original Chrysler 392-ci Hemi or the newer Chrysler 426-ci Race Hemi, both with iron blocks. Engine builder Ed Donovan designed and built the first aluminum Hemi block based on the 392-ci Chrysler. "Kansas" John Weibe was his first customer. He debuted it at the 1971 NHRA Supernationals, where he was the number one qualifier at 6.53 seconds, and was the only Top Fuel competitor to run in the 6.50-second range. In 1974, legendary engine builder Keith Black introduced an aluminum block engine based on the 426 Race Hemi. These aluminum blocks offered light weight and unparalleled strength. In 1974, Donovan introduced aluminum cylinder heads for the Hemi. Within five years, Top Fuel engine technology had made a shift from modified factory parts to specialized racing components.

As early as 1963, Garlits had experimented with wings and airfoils. When he first ran his rear engine car, he didn't have a rear wing. He added one, and soon so did every other competitor. The rear wing increased downforce and the cars ran quicker with them than without. Carl Olson and his partner Mike Kuhl built their first rear engine dragster in late 1971. In 1972, the pair won Top Fuel at the NHRA Winternationals. "We installed a wing on our car in early 1972 and immediately picked up a tenth of a second," recalls Olson. "The first run I ever made with a rear wing was at Bakersfield, California. With the wing, it was a completely different racecar. It was absolutely hooked up from the starting line to the finish line and was infinitely easier to drive. It was so noticeable that I made a mental note to myself that I would *never* make another run down a drag strip without a rear wing." At the time, the knowledge of racecar aerodynamics was minimal. On a loose racetrack, the wing could be adjusted to grab a little more air and on a good track the wing would be leveled out. It was all done by guesswork.

Next page: Don Garlits set the drag racing world on its collective ear in 1975 when he shattered the 250-mile-per-hour barrier in *Swamp Rat 22.* In addition to setting the record, he won both the NHRA and IHRA points championships in 1975.

Compared to the rear engine Top Fuelers of today, Garlits' 1975 *Swamp Rat 22* car seems small and almost frail in construction. For safety reasons, Garlits added side view mirrors to this dragster.

By the mid-1970s, nearly every Top Fuel competitor was running an aluminum block. Two versions were used, one based on the old 392 Hemi and this one, based on the newer 426 Hemi. At that time, only one fuel pump was used to feed nitro to the injector and intake manifold. Horsepower for this engine was approximately 2,500.

Throughout the early 1970s, Don Garlits continued to refine, build, and race rear engine dragsters. In 1975 he was driving his *Swamp Rat XXII*. In addition to being in a struggle for both the IHRA (International Hot Rod Association) and NHRA points championship, Garlits had his eye on setting a new speed record of 250 miles per hour. For several years, Top Fuel dragsters had been nudging the 250-mile-per-hour mark, but no one had exceeded it. Garlits had posted a top speed of 249.30 four times during the 1975 season and was determined to break the record. The dramatic event would happen at the NHRA Supernationals that were held in Ontario, California, in October.

When Garlits arrived at the event, he had an engine stashed away that was the most powerful he had ever built. He also brought along a pair of slicks that, at 36 inches in diameter, were larger than any others. Garlits felt that the combination of the hot engine and larger-diameter tires would be enough to push his dragster over the 250-mile-per-hour mark.

In 1986, the late Gary Ormsby drove the Castrol-sponsored Top Fuel dragster. This is one of the streamlined versions that was tested in an effort to gain more speed. Drag racers found that downforce was more important than streamlining. ©Ron Lewis

On Friday night at his motel, Garlits swapped engines and fitted the special tires on his dragster. When he arrived at the track on Saturday, he was greeted by a rain shower. By the afternoon, the track was ready for qualifying. In 1975, competitors flipped a coin for lane choice. Garlits lost the coin toss and was assigned the lane in which a car had just oiled down the track. The NHRA Safety Safari crew had done an excellent job of cleaning up the oil, but Garlits, like all serious drag racing competitors, would have chosen to run in a clean lane. When he stopped at the end of his burnout, Garlits noticed that there was still a dusting of rice ash on the track. Rice ash is used to absorb oil. Garlits also noticed that his competitor wasn't in the other lane. He had shut his car off and Garlits would be making a single run. When he got back to the starting line, Garlits signaled to the starter, Buster Couch, that he wanted to switch to the now vacant good right lane, but Couch refused to let him switch. Garlits had second thoughts about trying for the record. "I didn't want to do it," Garlits confides. "This was a killer engine that was shakin' the ground. I didn't want to go out there and spin the tires and blow it up." As he staged the car, a voice in the back of his head told him that he *had* to make the run. "I pulled up there and I just kinda stepped down on it," says Garlits. "The front end came up about a foot off the ground and the front wheels never turned—they just stayed stationary in the air." Garlits' car had a two-speed transmission and he wanted to get through this rice ash before he shifted into high. "I just ran it out in low gear as far as it would go—it was just screamin'. It still hadn't touched the front wheels down yet and it's still goin' straight." Once it shifted into high gear, the front wheels came down with noticeable whiffs of smoke because at that point, the

car was already running over 200 miles per hour. "It went through 250.69 miles per hour and 5.63 seconds. We got the record! It was the first car over 250." Garlits went on to win the event and become the 1975 NHRA Top Fuel Champion.

Throughout the 1970s and early 1980s, every Top Fuel dragster had some sort of rear wing, but Top Fuel rear wing technology took a big jump in 1984 when Joe Amato cantilevered the wing off of the rear of his dragster. At the time, everyone was running the wing on supports straight above the rear axle. Tim Richards was Amato's crew chief at the time. "Timmy was pretty smart and savvy," says Amato. "We spent some time talking to different people who were aerodynamic types. We were told that we were not using the element correctly." Everyone, including Amato, was using the rear wing as a spoiler and not as a true aerodynamic element. "We cantilevered it off backward and flattened the wing out so the wing became a *wing*," says Amato. The cantilever effect of moving the wing rearward multiplied the leverage and they also raised it up higher. "The next thing you know, bingo! I set the record at 264 miles per hour," exclaims Amato. "When we showed up and put the wing on, everybody laughed at us," recalls Amato. "Two weeks later, everybody had the same thing."

In the early 1990s, the Top Fuel class got a shot in the arm when two of the biggest names in drag racing moved from Funny Cars to Top Fuel. Kenny Bernstein had raced Top Fuel years before, but made his name in Funny Cars. Don Prudhomme started in Top Fuel, became a champion, went to Funny Cars, became a champion, and was returning to his dragster roots. These guys weren't moving to Top Fuel because the pickings were easy. The level of competition was at an all-time

In 1986, Don Garlits raced his *Swamp Rat 30*. It featured an enclosed cockpit and small 500x5 aircraft wheels on the front. Garlits rode the *Swamp Rat 30* to one of the most spectacular blowovers in drag racing history at the 1986 NHRA Summernationals at Englishtown, New Jersey. ©*Ron Lewis*

Darrell Gwynn was one of Top Fuel racings fastest rising stars in the 1980s. He made his Top Fuel debut in 1985 and won 18 NHRA events. His driving career was cut short by a bad accident while running in England in 1990. ©Ron Lewis

high with competitors like Gary Ormsby, Joe Amato, Darrell Gwynn, Shirley Muldowney, and Don Garlits tearing up the Top Fuel ranks. Ed "The Ace" McCulloch was another one of the Funny Car greats to make the switch to Top Fuel in the early 1990s. "All of the guys had gone from Funny Car to Top Fuel," says McCulloch. "To be quite frank, [John] Force was the only Funny Car guy I cared about. I didn't want to race Funny Cars. I wanted to go with the guys I raced against all my life." When McCulloch had the option of running Larry Minor's dragster, he jumped at the chance. For two years he drove the McDonalds-sponsored dragster that was tuned by Lee Beard. McCulloch continued his winning ways, as he won one of drag racing's biggest races, the 1992 U.S. Nationals in his Top Fuel dragster.

In 1992, one of drag racing's biggest records, the 300-mile-per-hour mark, fell to Kenny Bernstein. Several Top Fuel teams had been dancing around that number, but it was an elusive record. Many didn't care about the speed record and concentrated on winning rounds. "I know Bernstein was working at it," says Amato. "They were looking at speed. At the time, we were working on consistency and winning championships—not just at getting speed. It's a different mindset." It happened on March 20 at Gainesville, Florida, during qualifying. Bernstein had been fast, but was not number one. As he rocketed through the traps he knew he was on a good run. "It really felt good, but I had no idea that it ran 300," recalls Bernstein. As he was turning off the track at the end, one of the workers was holding up three fingers. Bernstein was dejected thinking he only qualified third after such a good run. As he was climbing out of the car, he was told by one of the jubilant workers, "You went 300 miles per hour!" Bernstein's official speed that day was 301.70 miles per hour. "It was a great honor to accomplish it and it meant a lot to us," says Bernstein. "My crew—they did it. I just went along for the ride." Working on Bernstein's record breaker were Top Fuel tuning experts Wes

Cerny and Dale Armstrong. It was their work on the fuel curve and magnetos that made the magic happen. To prove the first 300-mile-per-hour pass wasn't a fluke, Bernstein repeated the speed that year at both Indianapolis and Englishtown, New Jersey. For the record, Doug Herbert was the second Top Fuel driver to exceed 300 miles per hour with a pass of 301.60 on February 13, 1993, at Pomona. Within a year, several Top Fuel drivers would be clicking off their first 300-mile-per-hour pass.

By 1995, speeds of 300 miles per hour were commonplace in Top Fuel. But, to reach those speeds, most competitors were running nitro percentages of 99 to 100 percent. In the late 1990s, a series of devastating engine explosions had the sanctioning bodies looking at ways to keep the engines in one piece, and still provide a good show for the fans. For the 2000 season, both the NHRA and IHRA took a bold step and limited the percentage of nitro in Top Fuel (and Funny Car) to 90 percent. Crew chiefs scrambled to make up for the lost power. What at first appeared to be something that would hurt the sport eventually helped. Engines were staying together, the cars were running faster than ever, and the fans were treated to the fastest side-by-side racing on earth.

Two of the top drag racers of all time, Joe Amato (foreground) and Don Prudhomme are caught in a 1991 side-by-side race. At this time, Top Fuel dragsters were running in the high 4-second range, at speeds just under 300 miles per hour. ©Ron Lewis

The engine in a Top Fuel dragster is capable of developing over 6,000 horsepower. It's limited to 500 cubic inches and must be based on an automotive design. The engine of choice is an all-aluminum design based on the Chrysler Hemi.

Anatomy of a
Modern Top Fuel
Dragster

Today's Top Fuel racecar represents a 30-year evolution of the rear

engine dragster. Most of the technology evolved by trial and

error, developed by average guys with above average mechanical

ability. Seat-of-the-pants engineering has been the hallmark of drag racing

since day one. Today, computers play a big part in the performance of

the Top Fuel dragsters—not by controlling the car's systems, but by

recording reams of data on what takes place in the 4.5 seconds it takes to

run the quarter. This data, along with years of experience, allows the

crew chiefs to tune the engine and clutch actuation system for maxi-

mum performance.

The engine used in a Top Fuel dragster is the same basic engine that powers a nitro Funny Car. A Top Fuel dragster is faster and quicker, because it is 200 pounds lighter than a Funny Car. (A Top Fuel dragster must weigh 2,175 pounds, including the driver, after each run.) Top Fuel dragsters have less aerodynamic drag and better traction than Funny Cars because of their weight distribution.

Chassis

As speeds increased and elapsed times lowered, the dragster chassis continued to get longer. Today, Top Fuel dragsters are restricted to a wheelbase of 180 to 300 inches. Every competitor in Top Fuel runs a chassis with a 300-inch wheelbase. Longer wheelbase chassis are easier to fine-tune for maximum traction and stability. The material used in the construction of a dragster frame is 4130 chrome moly tubing. Chrome moly tubing provides the best combination of light weight, strength, and flexibility (at speed, a Top Fuel chassis will curve upward between the axles as much as 8 inches). All chrome moly welds must be done using the TIG heliarc process (the best and strongest method). To provide maximum protection for the driver, sanctioning

Today's Top Fuel dragster is the fastest accelerating racecar in the world. In 4.5 seconds it can go from a standing start to 330 miles per hour. They run faster mile-per-hour speeds and quicker elapsed times than nitro Funny Cars because they have better traction and better aerodynamics. All Top Fuel dragsters have a 300-inch wheelbase and are constructed from chrome moly tubing. At the end of a run, the car, with driver, must weigh no more than 2,175 pounds.

Ground effects are not allowed on Top Fuel dragsters. What is permitted is a set of airfoils which consist of small front wings, side deflector plates in front of the headers, and a large rear wing. In the past, attempts have been made to aerodynamically streamline the cars, but most of these experiments have been unsuccessful.

bodies clearly define the requirements for construction of the roll cage. These requirements are designed to build a structure that will protect the driver from an impact at any angle. The inside surfaces of the bars that surround the driver must be padded for added protection. Dragster chassis cannot be plated, but they can be painted. Grinding of the welds is not allowed because it can make a bad weld look good. Chassis must be inspected each year by the sanctioning bodies and have a certification sticker affixed.

A Top Fuel dragster does not have a conventionally sprung suspension. The rear axle is solidly mounted to the frame. Up front, small A-arms are mounted to the frame with adjustable Heim joints. The front tread width is restricted to a 26-inch minimum. The front wheels are restricted to a diameter of 17 inches, and all Top Fuel dragsters run Goodyear 17x3 tires in the front and Goodyear slicks in the rear (see sidebar).

Aerodynamics plays an important part in Top Fuel dragsters. Unfortunately, it's difficult to get accurate data from wind tunnel tests on a Top Fuel dragster. Traditional automotive wind tunnels are unable to simulate 300-mile-per-hour speeds. While the wind tunnels made for aircraft can reach speeds of 300 miles per hour, they don't have a moving ground plane. Therefore, any results in such a test would be inaccurate.

Slicks: Smoke 'Em if You Got 'Em

Racing slicks have come a long way in 50 years. Early drag racers used bald street tires, because they found that the lack of tread gave them the best adhesion to dry pavement. Drag racers adapted sprint car tires because of their almost treadless design. Tire recappers were creating slicks by adding new rubber to old tire carcasses. While these tires were wide and free of tread, the rubber compounds were not designed for maximum traction. It wasn't until 1958 that the first purpose-built drag slick was manufactured and sold by M&H Tire Company. Further development by M&H, as well as many other tire manufacturers, contributed greatly to increasing speeds and lowering elapsed times in all drag racing classes.

Today, Top Fuel cars have only one choice for tires—Goodyear Eagle Dragway Specials. In the catalog, they're officially listed as 36x17.5x16 with a suggested retail price of $480 each. These tires are a "bead lock" design. This means that a portion of the wheel rim clamps around the bead of the tire for positive retention. These tires are designed to yield to rotational speed and change in diameter and width as the speed of the car increases. The static dimensions of the tire are 36 inches in diameter, with a 17.5-inch tread width and a circumference of 114 inches. (NHRA rules allow a tire to have an 18-inch width and 118-inch circumference.) When running at speed, the tire expands to a diameter of 5 feet, while the tread width shrinks to 10 to 12 inches. This change in size has the effect of a variable gear ratio. At low speeds, where tire traction is most critical, the tire is shorter in height and has a wider cross-section. The wrinkling action of the tire's sidewall upon acceleration from a dead stop is called "wrapping" or "wrapping up." This is where the rim wants to turn faster than the tire and the sidewalls give, wrinkling the sidewall severely. At the hit of the throttle, when the tire is wrapped, its contact patch with the ground is as long as it is wide, giving maximum tire contact to the pavement and maximum traction. As the car accelerates away from the starting line, the tire quickly changes shape. It's during this transition from short and squat to tall and thin that the phenomenon of tire shake happens. Tire shake occurs when the tire does not unwrap smoothly and starts to roll over itself and slap the ground, violently shaking the car. As the speed increases, the tire's diameter grows,

effectively changing the gear ratio and allowing the car to reach a higher speed. Even though the tread width becomes narrower at higher speeds, the coefficient of traction is equalized by the thousands of pounds of downforce generated by the rear wing.

Goodyear has successfully engineered an amazing tire for drag racing. Two different compounds are offered by Goodyear for its Top Fuel slicks: the older compound, which Goodyear calls D2; and the newer D2A compound, which is more heat resistant and has improved wear characteristics. Most Top Fuel teams prefer the D2A compound tires. Tire pressures on a Top Fuel slick are between 5.5 to 7 psi when the tire is cold. During a burnout, the tire's temperature is around 120 degrees. A short burnout will get the tire up to temperature. The main purpose of the burnout is not so much to heat up the tire, but to clean off the old compound on the tire's surface. The burnout is important for traction, because it lays down fresh rubber on the track. Long burnouts do nothing more than prematurely wear out the tires, but burnouts look cool. After a full quarter-mile

This fresh set of Goodyear slicks has been mounted and will soon be turned into clouds of white smoke and 300-mile-per-hour speeds. The rims are a "bead lock" design that clamp around the tire's bead for positive retention. Without the bead lock feature, the tires would spin off of the rims.

pass, the slick's temperature ranges between 250 and 400 degrees. The tread depth on a new Goodyear slick is approximately 0.20 inch at the tire's center. Goodyear's Top Fuel slicks are bias construction. The rubber compounds of these tires contribute less than 1 percent to the tire's structure. Almost all of the structure comes from the fabric carcass, most of which is nylon. The elastic properties of the nylon allow the tire to "wrap up" during the launch and "grow" at the top end. Hats off to Goodyear for making a tire that allows Top Fuel cars to run the quarter in 4.5 seconds at speeds over 330 miles per hour.

Today's Top Fueler is as aerodynamically clean as it can be, considering the large engine it must house. The dragster has a small frontal area and the only add-ons are for downforce. Streamlined bodies with enclosed cockpits have been tried, but the experiments never conclusively proved their effectiveness. Streamlined parts or fairings on the front wheels are not allowed. They have been tried in the past and tend to work like a rudder on an airplane, overcontrolling the car at high speeds. Ground effects are also not allowed on Top Fuel cars. This includes any skirts, belly pans, or tunnels that have an effect on downforce. The placement of certain "airfoils" is permitted. On the front, small wings keep the nose down at speed; and on the side of the body, just behind the cockpit, are deflector plates that help direct air up over the rear tires.

A large wing is securely mounted on the back of each Top Fuel dragster. This wing provides between 4,000 and 8,000 pounds of downforce on the last half of the track, commonly referred to as the "top end." Without this downforce, the rear tires would not be able to provide traction at the top end. NHRA and IHRA rules limit Top Fuel dragsters to a single wing, but the wing can have up to a maximum of three elements. The total number of allowable square inches of airfoil rearward of the front axle is 1,500. Maximum height of the rear wing from its rear edge to the ground is 90 inches. Its trailing edge cannot extend more than 50 inches behind the centerline of the rear axle. Spill plates at the ends of the wing are allowed, but they can be no larger than 22 by 22 inches. Attachment points are limited to the chassis. Rules forbid attachment of the wing support struts to the engine or bellhousing. Rules also forbid any device that controls the wing's angle of attack during the run. Its setting is made prior to a run.

The rear wing on a Top Fuel dragster provides up to 8,000 pounds of downforce. The wing's maximum height is 90 inches, and its rear edge cannot extend more than 50 inches behind the centerline of the rear axle. The wing can only be adjusted prior to a run. Rules forbid any device that controls the wing's angle of attack during a run.

With the right rear tire and some of the body panels removed, the network of chrome moly tubing that makes up the chassis and the rear axle can be seen. Top Fuel dragsters only have rear brakes, but they are gigantic! Top Fuel dragsters are limited to a 3.20 rear end ratio that is housed in a large aluminum rear axle. The large vertical struts are for the rear wing.

Top Fuel dragsters have an onboard computer that collects data during the run. The control of the fuel, clutch, and ignition timing is done with a series of pneumatic timers. Each timer is preset to perform a specific function at a certain point in the run. Here, John Smith, crew chief of the *Fram*-sponsored dragster, is adjusting the timers.

With the body panel removed from the side of the cockpit of Mike Dunn's *New York Yankees* dragster, the accelerator pedal can be seen. It was milled from billet aluminum and powder coated black. It has a small aluminum heel plate and a metal retaining hoop over the toe. Attached to the frame under the pedal is a circular metal stop. Attached to the stop is the air switch that initiates the car's pneumatic timers. When the pedal is fully depressed, the switch is actuated. Total pedal travel is approximately 1 inch for 6,000 horsepower.

On a track with poor traction at the top end, the car's rear wing will have more downforce dialed in to keep the tires from spinning as the car goes through the traps.

The dragster body is a combination of sheet aluminum and composites. Body panels are attached with Dzus fasteners for easy removal. A small wraparound wind screen is placed in front of the driver. Behind the driver's roll cage is a plate designed to separate the driver from any flying components from an exploding engine. If it's made of aluminum, this plate must be 1/8 inch thick. If it's made out of steel or titanium, 1/16 inch is acceptable. The fuel tank (12 to 15 gallons) is placed as far forward as possible. The forward placement of the tank precludes the addition of ballast to keep the nose down upon launch. Fuel is delivered through a large diameter aluminum pipe that runs from the tank, under the driver's seat, to the engine's fuel pumps. There is no pump in the tank to feed fuel back to the engine; it's simply pushed rearward by the G-force of the car's acceleration. A small fuel tank vent on the front of the body has a mild ram-air effect to assist in the flow of fuel. On the back of the dragster, under the wing, is a catch-can for engine blowby. This can, which is connected to the engine's valve covers, is commonly called a "puke tank" because it collects the oil the engine throws off. Also in the rear is the oil reservoir tank for the engine's dry sump system. On the rear are two parachutes used to slow the car from high speeds. Each parachute has a separate mounting point on the frame and each has its own release in the cockpit. Because the engine is behind the driver and the cockpit is open, no onboard fire suppression system is required on a Top Fuel dragster.

Computers are not allowed to actuate any system on a Top Fuel dragster, although

Pit work on a Top Fuel dragster goes on at all hours of the day and night. There are no time-outs in drag racing. If a car cannot make its designated time to run, the round is forfeited.

computers are allowed to record data that can be analyzed after the run. Pneumatic timers control the clutch application, fuel distribution, and ignition timing. These timers are located in front of the driver's compartment. An air bottle provides compressed air to actuate these timers. A 3-second sequence of over 20 timed events (5–10 clutch, 10–12 for fuel, and 3–4 for ignition timing) starts when the driver fully steps on the throttle and actuates an air switch under the accelerator pedal. The crew chief determines the sequence of events to be controlled by each of the pneumatic timers and sets each of them to perform its function at a certain point in the run.

Engine

Today's Top Fuel dragster engine must be based on an automotive design. Sanctioning body rules require it to be a 90-degree (angle between cylinder banks) V-8 and run a single camshaft (no overhead cams). Cubic inch displacement is restricted to a minimum of 490 and a maximum of 500. There are no restrictions on the head design other than there must be only two valves per cylinder. Superchargers are allowed, but turbochargers are not. The engine that is best suited to the rules is a supercharged Hemi-style engine, the same basic engine that has powered Top Fuel dragsters for over 40 years.

While today's Top Fuel engine resembles the old-style Hemi, it's eons ahead in technology

Cylinder heads for today's Top Fuel dragsters are all milled from billet aluminum. This head has had the rocker shafts removed. It's resting on its intake ports, but the exhaust headers are still attached. The tube running the length of the head provides fuel to the two nozzles located behind each intake valve.

The engine blocks for Top Fuel dragsters are made from aluminum and are fitted with cast-iron cylinder sleeves. This particular block has been milled from a solid billet, but there are others that are either forged or cast. The number one piston has been fitted and the crew member is checking it with a dial indicator. The studs sticking out of the block are used for cylinder head attachment. The 12-point fasteners on the lower sides of the block are attached to the main bearing caps.

and horsepower. In the early 1960s, fuel-burning Hemi engines were producing approximately 1,000 horsepower. Today's Top Fuel engines produce 6,000 horsepower, and some estimates are as high as 8,000. Inventive crew chiefs have been able to fine-tune fuel and ignition curves through careful analysis of onboard data recorders to produce these horsepower numbers. The materials used in these engines have improved enough to withstand the massive explosions that occur in each cylinder.

Cylinder blocks in today's Top Fuel dragsters are constructed from aluminum and are designed for drag racing only. Cast-aluminum blocks are made by several compa-

This is the business end of a Top Fuel cylinder head. All combustion chambers are exactly the same size. The intake valves (lower side) are 2.40 inches in diameter and the exhaust valves are 1.90 inches in diameter. The threaded holes on either side of the valves are for the sparkplugs. Around the combustion chamber on the face of the head is a small recess cut for a stainless wire that seals against the copper head gasket.

nies and have been popular with competitors for decades, but the latest technology is a forged-aluminum block. Forged blocks are much stronger, but are slightly heavier, as the material is more dense. The cylinder blocks used in Top Fuel competition do not have water jackets like those on passenger cars. Since the duration of the run is short, a cooling system is not necessary. Inserted into each cylinder is a specially made ductile cast-iron sleeve. These sleeves are made using a centrifugal casting process and are carefully machined. To obtain a legal displacement of between 490 and 500 cubic inches, almost all Top Fuel teams use a 4.19-inch bore with a 4.50-inch stroke, which equals 496 cubic inches. Crew chiefs call this particular 4.50-inch crankshaft a "3/4 stroker." Another bore

and stroke combination of 4.25-inch bore with a stroke of 4.38 is available with a "5/8 stroker" crank. Eddie Hill was the last to successfully run this combination. Aluminum pistons and connecting rods are used for their light weight and strength. The crankshaft weighs 79 pounds and is made from billet chrome-vanadium steel. Teams limit the amount of runs on each crankshaft to prevent catastrophic engine failures. All Top Fuel teams run a dry sump oiling system.

Hemi-style cylinder heads for Top Fuel dragsters are machined from billet aluminum. These heads do not have complex water passages or intricate ports like those on a passenger car. The intake and exhaust ports have a large cross-section, are short in length, and are almost straight. The intake valves are 2.40 inches in

This young lad watches in wonder as the *Winston* Top Fuel dragster is being unloaded from its transporter. The car is stored without its wing in the top section of the trailer. A dolly is fitted to the front section of the frame to allow the front wheels to dangle over the ramp.

The fuel injector on this dragster's engine is made out of carbon fiber. Rules restrict the opening size to 65 square inches. The linkage on the right connects to the driver's accelerator pedal. There are only three fuel lines fed into each side of the injector. Between the fuel lines are three air bleeds that are fitted with plugs. The crew chief can fine-tune the engine's idle by adding or removing a plug, thereby changing the air-fuel ratio.

diameter and are made of titanium. The exhaust valves are 1.90 inches in diameter and are made of Inconel. Shaft-mounted rocker arms actuate the valves. These rocker arms are connected via pushrods to a single long-duration roller camshaft. Attached to the heads are a set of zoomie exhaust headers. The force of the exhaust from these headers helps create additional downforce for traction.

Sitting on top of the engine is a Roots-style supercharger (also known as a blower). These superchargers are similar to the 6-71 GMC superchargers used in the 1960s. The maximum size allowed on a Top Fueler today is a 14-71 with a 19-inch-long case and a maximum rotor cavity diameter of 5.84 inches. Internally, there are two three-bladed rotors with a helical shape. These rotors are inter-meshed like two three-toothed gears. They are synchronized by two external gears that prevent the rotors from coming in contact with each other. As these rotors spin, they compress the air that is fed into the engine's cylinders. The super-charger is belt-driven off of the crankshaft and can spin as fast as 12,000 rpm. By changing pulley sizes, the crew chief can change the speed of the blower, increasing the amount of boost the supercharger generates. This increased blower speed above one-to-one is called "overdrive" and is defined as a percentage. The AHRA allows a maximum of 25 percent over-drive. While the NHRA has no limit, NHRA competitors typically run 40 per-cent overdrive. A "burst panel" is located on the intake manifold. This metallic panel is designed to open at a certain pressure that would develop in case of a backfire, thereby preventing a cata-strophic supercharger explosion. On top of the supercharger is the fuel injector. Its opening size is limited to 65 square inches. The throttle blades are actuated by a cable to the driver's right foot. A removable throttle stop is attached to the cable to limit the amount of throttle opening during a burnout.

Each cylinder has two sparkplugs, and each plug is lit by its own magneto. Two magnetos are used because of the massive amount of fuel pouring into each cylinder. The magnetos used in Top Fuel send 1,200 milliamps of current to the plugs. (The average passenger car's distributor, in good tune, has an output of 30 milliamps.) Both magnetos are connected by a cog belt to ensure they are timed identically. In addition, some crew chiefs also have a mechanical connection between the magnetos to reduce vibration. Ignition timing is varied during the run by a system of air solenoids. Timing is a critical component of the tune-up, and crew chiefs work in 1/2-degree increments for optimum performance.

The fuel system on a Top Fuel dragster is the key to its performance. Once crew chiefs found that they could pump massive amounts

With a valve cover removed, the Hemi's twin rocker shafts can be seen. The upper set is for the intake valves and the lower set is for the exhaust valves. The exhaust valve train bears the brunt of the workload, because it must open the valves against tremendous cylinder pressure. Also visible is the fuel system plumbing to the intake manifold ports and into the cylinder head for the down nozzles.

of nitromethane into an engine, they did everything they could to increase fuel flow. Mounted on the front of the engine are two fuel pumps that can produce fuel pressures of 500 to 600 psi at a flow rate of 75 gallons per minute. Both pumps are adjustable from the driver's seat. Braided stainless lines are routed from the pumps up to the barrel valve, which is mounted on the injector. The barrel valve has a mechanical link to the injector's butterflies. As the butterflies open, more fuel flows to the engine through the barrel valve. Only a small amount of fuel is fed into the injector hat. This fuel keeps the supercharger lubricated. Most of the fuel is routed to the intake manifold nozzles and 16 pairs of "down" nozzles, located within the cylinder head's intake ports just behind the intake valves. During a run, a Top Fuel dragster consumes approximately 1 gallon of fuel per second. The starting process, burnout, and staging consume approximately 5 to 7 gallons of fuel. At idle, a Top Fuel engine uses 4 gallons of nitro per minute—that's a gallon every 15 seconds. An entire

Top Fuel dragsters use a five-disk clutch with four floater plates. Here, two complete clutch packs are waiting their turn to go racing. The clutch is designed to slip at the start to allow the tires to bite into the racing surface. At approximately half-track, the clutch timers cause the clutch to be fully engaged.

Maintenance on Don Prudhomme's *Miller Lite* Top Fuel dragster is handled by a team of experts. After the engine has been warmed in the pits, the oil is changed, because it has been contaminated with nitromethane. The crewman on the left in the foreground is adding fresh oil, while one crewman on each side checks the valve lash.

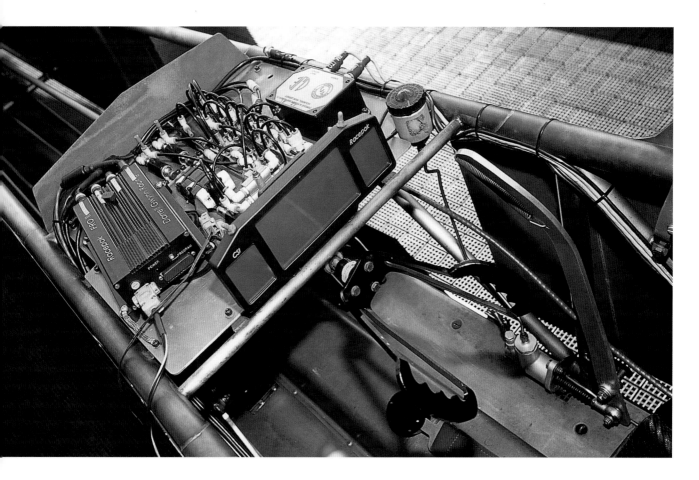

The cockpit of a Top Fuel dragster is extremely simple. The lever to the right is the brake handle. In the far upper right are the two parachute release handles. In front of the driver is an aluminum butterfly steering wheel. This particular car has an liquid-crystal display (LCD) digital driver's display. This is used by the crew chief to check engine rpm before the run; in a 4.5-second run, the driver doesn't have time to check the display. In front of the display panel is the data-recording computer and some of the solenoids.

run, from the time the engine starts to the turn-off at the end of the track, may consume as many as 15 gallons of fuel. At $30 per gallon, this equates to $450—just for fuel.

Behind the engine is the 10.5-inch-diameter clutch. It has 18 adjustable fingers. Top Fuel dragsters can run either a four- or five-disc clutch, but today, the five-disc is the accepted standard. The clutch is enclosed in a titanium flywheel shield. Between the clutch and rear end is a reverser. The reverser is technically not a transmission. It has a set of planetary gears that, when engaged, reverses the output to the rear axle. This allows the car to back up after a burnout. The only rear end ratio allowed is 3.20:1.

Cockpit Controls

The driver of a Top Fuel car is seated in a semireclined position. Unlike a Funny Car driver, who must look around the engine, the view forward in a Top Fuel dragster is unobstructed. The seat is usually constructed out of carbon fiber and has no covering. Drivers want to feel the car as much as possible, and any seat covering filters out the "feel" of the car. A sturdy set of five-point seat belts holds the driver snugly in place. The driver's arms are outstretched to reach the small aluminum butterfly steering wheel. On the floor to the right is the accelerator pedal and on the left is the clutch. There is no brake pedal. Brakes are applied using a vertical brake handle to the driver's right. On certain occasions, to control wheel spin or tire shake, the driver might apply the hand brake while accelerating. On the left side of the cockpit are two levers which turn the fuel pumps on and off. On the right side are two levers for the parachutes. Somewhere within easy reach of the driver is a kill switch for the mags. This switch has a cover that protects it from being accidentally tripped. There is another lever in the cockpit that controls the reverser. Most Top Fuel drivers do not want or need any other controls or gauges.

Behind the titanium bellhousing is a small reverser. The reverser allows a Top Fuel dragster to back up after a burnout.

Driver's Equipment

Long gone are the days when a Top Fuel driver wore a T-shirt or a leather jacket to sit behind a fuel-burning engine. Today, each Top Fuel driver is required to wear a long list of items for his or her safety. A full, seven-layer Nomex driving suit is required. Top Fuel drivers

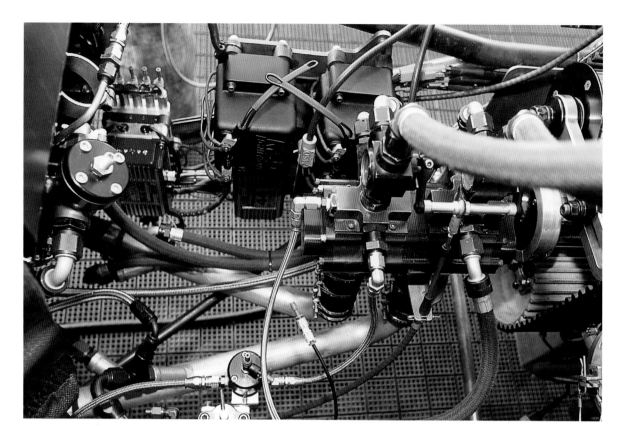

The massive amount of fuel pumped into a Top Fuel engine is what allows it to produce so much power. Located on the front of the engine, these pumps take fuel from the fuel tank's two large aluminum feed lines and pressurize it to 600 psi before feeding it to the engine's nozzles.

can be seen in two different styles of driving suits. The first is the one piece jump suit that is similar to what CART (Championship Auto Racing Teams) and NASCAR (National Association for Stock Car Auto Racing) drivers wear. Also allowed for Top Fuel drivers is a two-piece Nomex suit of pants and jacket. Nomex gloves and shoes or boots are required. Each driver must wear a full-face helmet. Some drivers tape the sides of their visors, as if wearing blinders. This is to keep the car in the other lane out of their field of

Opposite: Gary Scelzi has hopped up on the roll bar of his *Winston*-sponsored dragster, prior to sliding down into the cockpit. All Top Fuel drivers must wear a full-face helmet similar to the one he is wearing. The attachment on the front of the helmet is for a strap that helps to counteract the acceleration G-forces. Around his neck are a padded collar and a HANS device that are designed to reduce head and neck injuries.

vision. If in view, some drivers unconsciously drive toward that car. Many drivers will tape the top edge of their visors to keep the sun out of their eyes. The tape usually displays the sponsor's name. Also required is a padded neck collar. This helps reduce head and neck injuries in case of an accident. A Nomex head sock or balaclava is required, unless the driver's helmet has a Nomex skirt. Many Top Fuel drivers also wear full Nomex long underwear and a few even have Nomex laces on their driving shoes, although these items are not required by the rules. Arm restraints are required to keep the driver's arms inside the car in case of a rollover. Another item not required by the rules, but used by several Top Fuel drivers, is a mouthpiece similar to the ones worn by professional boxers. Top Fuel driver Larry Dixon started to wear one at the advice of his father-in-law, who had been involved in a drag racing accident in a Pro-Stock Truck. "I thought I should," exclaims Dixon. "If you think about it, I don't know why you wouldn't. Football players wear them and they're not going 320 miles per hour when they hit." In Memphis, in 2000, both Dixon and Tony Schumacher were involved in serious race crashes. "Tony ruined his teeth and had to have caps on all

his teeth. My teeth and my mouthpiece were just fine through that whole deal. With so many things that happen, the last thing you want to think about is fixing your teeth." Since those two accidents, more Top Fuel and Funny Car drivers have started to wear a mouthpiece.

A recent safety innovation, initially developed for the drivers of open wheel racecars, is the HANS (Head And Neck Support) device. The HANS device reduces the whiplash movements of the driver's head during the rapid deceleration that occurs during an accident or when both chutes blossom at 330 miles per hour, generating 5 to 7 negative Gs. The first Top Fuel driver to try one was Gary Scelzi. "When you crash, your body does things that you can't believe," says Scelzi. "In fact, in a pedal, I've seen an in-car camera where the guy's head actually hit his chest and came back up." Scelzi first learned about it while watching a television piece on how CART and Formula One were going to make the device mandatory for their drivers. Scelzi went to Chip Ganassi's CART racecar shop in Indianapolis to get more information. The model Scelzi decided upon is a HANS Model-III, which is designed for the reclining position used by CART and Formula One drivers. At first he found the HANS somewhat awkward and uncomfortable, but he also conceded that all the other required safety equipment took some time to get used to. After eight runs wearing the HANS, Scelzi became a convert and an evangelist preaching its virtues. "It keeps my head from going so far forward and it's helped my neck and back injuries." Several Top Fuel and Funny Car drivers have started wearing the HANS device.

While in the staging lanes prior to a run, Kenny Bernstein, driver of the *Budweiser King* Top Fuel dragster, casually chats with one of his crew members. Bernstein is one of the drivers who wears a two-piece Nomex fire suit. At this point, he is only wearing the Nomex underwear, pants, and boots. Prior to getting in the car he will add the jacket, helmet, neck collar, and gloves.

Once Top Fuel driver Gary Scelzi is strapped in to his *Winston* dragster, he visualizes the race he's about to run. He also goes through a mental checklist of what he might have to do if things don't go perfectly. This might include pedaling the car if the tires smoke or pulling the chutes early if the engine blows.

Chapter 4

Driving a
Modern Top Fuel
Dragster

In the early days of Top Fuel racing, the driver did everything but drive the push truck. Today the driver's job is just to drive the car. Although some drivers mix the fuel and fill the car's tank and a few drivers might also pack the parachutes, most teams don't want their drivers distracted from the task at hand. They also don't want the driver to neglect a set of maintenance responsibilities because of a television interview.

According to the rules, the driver is required to sit in the car when it's test-fired in the pits. The engine is run to make sure that there are no leaks in the fuel or oil systems. During the test fire, the crew chief sets the timing. The test-fire procedure also includes seating the clutch. This is done to remove all microscopic high spots on the clutch disks and floater plates. Dick LaHaie, crew chief of Larry Dixon's *Miller Lite* car, prefers to have Dixon stab the throttle twice while holding the brake, with the clutch pedal fully released. "We feel as though we seat it the same way it leaves the starting line," says LaHaie. "We hit the throttle and it goes up to about 7,000 rpm." Other teams hold the engine at a lower rpm for a specific length of time.

With the car fully prepped for the first round of racing, it is towed into the staging lanes. The crew chiefs study the cars that are racing to get a feel for track adhesion and for which lane looks better. They also take periodic samplings of the track's temperature. Small changes can still be made to the car's tune-up and clutch settings while in the staging lanes. Also at this time, the drivers are getting physically and mentally prepared for the first round of racing. They are donning their fireproof driving suits and slipping on their helmet and gloves. Once fully suited, they are strapped into the car.

This is how Larry Dixon, NHRA's 1995 Rookie of the Year and driver of Don Prudhomme's *Miller Lite* dragster, describes his routine: "Maybe four or five pairs before I run, I start shutting down. Shutting everything out. You've got to flush out all the other distractions—who did what on the racetrack, who came by and said this or said that. You tend to what's at hand—the competition. When there's about three pairs ahead, I start putting on my equipment. Also at that time everybody goes through their routine right down to

Larry Dixon sits in the driver's seat of the *Miller Lite* dragster while the engine is test-fired in the pits. On the right, crew chief Dick LaHaie is making a final adjustment to the engine's tune-up. During this test firing, the clutch is seated. To do this, the driver holds the brake while stabbing the throttle once or twice.

In addition to driving the car, Larry Dixon and a few of the other Top Fuel drivers also have the responsibility of mixing the fuel and adding it to the car's tank. A cover is placed over the forward portion of the body, since nitromethane is also an excellent paint remover.

the guy who checks the air in the tires. You do everything repetitively so there's nothing you can forget or leave out. Even dumb stuff like putting on your safety equipment. The left glove goes on before the right glove, but you do it the same every single time. Some people think it's superstition or habit. But, if you do everything the exact same way every single time, it's something that you can put out of your mind. You'll know that you did it and did it right."

The routine continues when Dixon is strapped into the car. The same crewman straps him in every time and uses the same sequence for attaching and tightening the belts. Once in the car, Dixon continues to mentally focus in preparation for the run. "If there's a crowd around, I'll roll the visor down a little so no one can see. A lot of times I'll just close my eyes and visualize what's going to happen. If this happens, this is what I'm going to do; if that happens, this is what I'm going to do."

Gary Scelzi, driver of the Winston Top Fuel dragster and NHRA Top Fuel Champion in 1997, 1998, and 2000, describes his preparation this way: "I joke right up to the time I get into the car. In fact, when my guys are seating me in, I'll tell them to look at this girl over there with the big boobs. I try to break up the intensity. But when my guys are done strapping me in, I make the sign of the cross, rub the two pictures in my cockpit [Blaine Johnson, former driver of the car, and Scelzi's son, Dominick], and I'm all business—I don't want to be bothered. I don't want any fans to be leaning their head in there. Cameras don't bother me, because I'm not paying attention to them. Once I'm belted in, I'm in my own world."

As the cars are pushed onto the track and to their designated lane, the drivers see the

track and the thousands of fans in the stands. When given the signal to start the engine, the crew chief signals to the driver that it's time to fire it up. A stream of gasoline is fed into the injector from a plastic bottle. Gasoline is used to get the engine running, because nitromethane is difficult to fire off in a cold engine. Once the engine is running, the crew chief reaches down and trims the fuel pumps to feed nitro to the engine. When this is done, there is a noticeable change in the pitch and volume of the exhaust. The engine goes from a rumble to what is known in Top Fuel circles as a "cackle." Scelzi has this feeling when the engine starts: "I'm nervous. I'm edgy. I say to myself, 'You wanted this. You want to be the champ and now's the time to show your metal—there's no time to be scared—do what you do.' When that motor starts, I forget everything. I go into race mode." Three-time NHRA Top Fuel Champion and legendary driver Shirley Muldowney says, "One of the things I like about it most is the sound. It just does something to me. Not so much with the throttle down as when they fire the car—I love that sound. I feel very at home and safe in the car."

Once the engine is running, the crew chief and all crew members check the car for any leaks. There are no time-outs in drag racing. If there is a problem with the car, the engine must be shut down and the round is

When the call is made for the Top Fuel class, the cars are towed to the staging lanes. Here, both nitro Funny Cars and Top Fuel dragsters are awaiting their turn to run. It's during this time that the drivers will get suited up, and the crew chiefs might make a final change to the car's tune-up. It's also during this time that the drivers mentally prepare for the upcoming run.

The limited amount of room in a Top Fuel dragster's cockpit and the restricted visibility of the helmet make it necessary for one of the crew to help strap the driver in. Drivers usually tug at the safety belts once they are settled in to make the belts even tighter.

With the car ready to race, the driver is securely strapped into the seat, and the crew has attached the starter motor to the blower. The crewman on the left is squirting gasoline into the engine, while the crewman on the right is running the remote starter. Once the engine is running, its fuel pumps will be turned on to feed nitro to the engine.

Once the car is running and the crew chief is confident that all of the car's systems are OK, he will motion the driver ahead to roll into the "bleach box." This is an area of the track well behind the starting line that is kept watered down. The water cleans the tires and acts as a lubricant to help the tires spin easier on the burnout. Here Mike Dunn, driver of the *Yankees* Top Fuel dragster, has just rolled through the water and is about to put the throttle down.

forfeited. Once everything is checked, the driver is motioned ahead for the burnout. With no pressure on the accelerator, the driver eases out the clutch and rolls through the water to wet the tires so they will spin easily. A signal is given to the driver by one of the crew and the accelerator is depressed to start the burnout. A stop on the injector limits the throttle opening to a few degrees. The engine instantly spools up to 5,000 rpm and the rear tires start to spin. "My favorite part of the run is the burnout," says Scelzi. "That's when

Fans, drivers, and Goodyear sales reps love the burnout! A stop is placed on the throttle cable that limits the engine's rpm to approximately 5,000. Without the stop, it would be difficult for the driver to limit the powerful nitro-burning engine's rpm.

you're smoking the tires and you've got 6,000 horsepower at your control and you're just havin' fun." The driver's job is to stay in the throttle for the same amount of time each time he or she does a burnout and then to get out of the throttle and roll out to the same spot on the track. This critically timed routine is designed to control the amount of fuel burned. Nitromethane weighs 10 pounds a gallon and the fuel tank is at the front of the car. The burn rate at idle is 4 gallons a minute. "Every 15 seconds extra that you're doing things different, you're taking 10 pounds of weight off, or adding 10 pounds of weight to,

the front end of the car," says Dixon. "When we make a front end weight change, we'll make it in 2 1/2-pound increments." This is why racers will get upset when a competitor takes too long to get through his starting routine.

When the car is stopped at the end of the burnout, the driver pushes in the clutch and engages the reverser. Without adding any throttle, the clutch is eased out and the car backs toward the starting line. Shortly after it starts its rearward roll, one of the crew members moves into the driver's field of vision in front of the car and signals with his arms the direction in which the driver should steer the

Burnouts are done to clean and add a little heat to the tires. The burnout also adds rubber to the track surface, which enhances traction.

car. The driver is being directed to place the car's rear tires on the best location on the starting line, which may not be in the tracks of rubber that were just laid down. "The whole time they're telling me where they want the rear tires, I'm concentrating on the front tires to make sure I'm aimed straight," says Dixon. "If the front end's not pointed down the center of the lane, you're not going to go down the center of the lane. In the first 150 to 200 feet of the run, you can't rely on steering the car, because the front end is usually in the air, or it's real light to where you can't even steer it." Driving a 300-inch wheelbase car in reverse is made even more difficult because of the amount of castor designed into the front suspension. The excessive castor helps keep the car straight at 300 miles per hour, but makes backing a Top Fuel dragster a tricky job. Occasionally, when backing too fast, the front wheels will start to wobble. To end the wobble, the driver must stop the car, and then slowly continue to back up.

Once the car is stopped behind the starting line, the driver pushes in the clutch and disengages the reverser. The crew again goes over the car, resetting the clutch, cleaning the rear tires, and visually checking for anything that could be a problem. The crew chief makes a final adjustment to the engine to get it set at a specific rpm, usually around 2,500. This adjustment may be a slight mechanical change to the barrel valve linkage on the injector, or the removal or addition of one or more small plugs in the injector hat that provide air bleeds. The crew chief also removes the stop that restricts the throttle opening during the burnout. Once satisfied that the car is ready, the crew chief motions the car forward and stops it when its front wheels are near the pre-stage beam. It's at this point that the car is solely in the hands of the driver.

"When I'm ready to race, I'll roll into the pre-stage beam," says Dixon. "When I'm ready to stage the car, I turn the fuel completely on." This is done by moving both cockpit fuel pump levers to the full ON position. This is often called "doubling up," because both pumps are fully activated. This adds an additional gallon of nitro per minute

A Day at Drag Racing School

In the course of my interviews with Gary Scelzi and Larry Dixon, they both mentioned that they had attended Frank Hawley's Drag Racing School to either learn how to drive a dragster or to refine their driving skills. Many of today's best Funny Car and Top Fuel drivers have attended Hawley's school. Frank Hawley is a two-time NHRA Funny Car champ and has driven every type of drag racing car, including Top Fuel. He opened his first Drag Racing School in Gainesville, Florida, in 1985. By 1996, the demand on the West Coast was great enough for him to start classes at Pomona. Hawley annually averages 1,000 drivers, who attend several types of courses for many types of drag racing cars and motorcycles. With this track record, there must be something there for me to investigate! After a quick call to the school—I was enrolled.

To get my feet wet, I decided upon the *Dragster Adventure I* program. This is a beginner's program designed to give the student a chance to do two burnouts and make two 1/8-mile passes in a 700-horsepower rear engine dragster. The program starts with 1 1/2 hours of classroom time during which safety is stressed. Every step of what the student will do is explained in detail. Then it's down to the track to get suited up. A full Nomex driver's suit is provided, along with neck collar, full-face helmet, and gloves. The cars are typical of those that would run in NHRA's Super Comp class. They are approximately 16 feet long and could run the quarter in 8.5 seconds at 160 miles per hour. For this class, the throttle is restricted to limit the 1/8-mile elapsed time to 7 seconds and the speed to 100 miles per hour. Plenty fast for a first-time dragster driver!

When my turn came, I tried to walk to the car with a "Top Fuel" swagger, as if I'd done this a million times before. I'm sure my swagger resembled a tentative shuffle, as my heart was in my throat and I was starting to sweat bullets. A staff member helps the students get seated and properly strapped in. Then you get the signal to start the engine. As the 700-horsepower big-block Chevy burbles away, it slightly rocks the chassis—I'm starting to feel more comfortable. The first big challenge is getting the long-wheelbase car turned and lined up properly in the lane. You don't want to look stupid and start off with a bad turn. Once in the lane, the first thing I noticed was that the rear engine dragster gives you an excellent view of the track. The instructor motions you ahead through the water box and signals you to stop, then he signals you to do the burnout. I stab the throttle

Jack Beckman, instructor at the Frank Hawley Drag Racing School, gives a student the thumbs-up to let the driver know that everything is OK for an upcoming pass. At the school, Top Fuel greenhorns and anxious journalists can have the thrill of driving a dragster in a highly controlled environment.

and the big Chevy engine jumps to life. As the rpm increase, I can feel the tires growing, lifting the rear of the car. This is really cool!

After I stopped the car, the instructor motioned me ahead to just short of the pre-stage beam. I use the brake to inch ahead and get the car staged. The tree blinks and I'm on the gas! There is not an immense kick at the start, just a strong steady pull. At about 400 feet I realized that I had a death grip on the wheel and I backed off the throttle. We were instructed to have a light grip to easily maintain control. Coming back on the return road after that first run I was more relaxed and had stopped sweating. I was really looking forward to my next run. On my second run, I took it the full 1/8 mile under power and felt comfortable. As I turned onto the return road, I could hear the crowd cheering. I could see Wally Parks smiling in the distance. I could see the beautiful trophy girl with two big trophies

in her hand: one for Top Eliminator and the other for top speed. I could . . . Wait a minute. The school's crew is waving me over. I've made my two passes and have to let someone else have some fun. I wished I had signed up for the *Adventure II* program that lets you take these cars the full quarter. I've driven down the quarter-mile many times, but I've never had as much fun as I did in this class. It was bitchin'!

For more information about how you could have the drag racing thrill of a lifetime, contact:

Frank Hawley's Drag Racing School
P.O. Box 484
La Verne, CA 91750
(888) 901-7223
www.frankhawley.com

As the engine spools up for the burnout, the rear tires grow in diameter and raise the rear of the car. During the burnout, the driver's job is to keep the car straight, get out of the throttle at a predetermined point, and smoothly stop the car.

to the engine. Those standing near the starting line hear a slight drop in engine rpm and see an increased wet nitro mist coming out of the exhaust. "I'll take my foot completely off the clutch," says Dixon. "Now I have to hold the car in place with the brake and then I basically brake-drive the car into the beams." Once fully staged, the driver's right hand is gripping the brake handle, the left hand is on the steering wheel, the left foot is completely off the clutch, both eyes are glued to the lights on the tree, and the right foot is itching to nail the throttle.

When both cars are staged, the track starter initiates the starting sequence. In the professional ranks, the Christmas tree simultaneously flashes all six (three on each side) yellow lights for four-tenths of a second before the green lights are lit. The idea is to leave before you actually see the green. A good reaction time can win a race over a quicker and faster car. Drivers continually work on their starting technique.

At the hit of the throttle, the engine instantly spools up to approximately 8,000 rpm. (Depending on track conditions, the rpm will vary between 7,800 and 8,300 rpm.) When the accelerator pedal is fully depressed, it trips an air valve that starts the timers that adjust timing, clutch, and fuel management.

As the torque is applied to the rear tires, they flatten out on the track and the car starts to move. "It's 3.5 Gs on the hit," says Scelzi. "Then about a second into the run, it's up to 5 Gs as the clutch starts coming in. It's pulling harder 100 feet off the starting line than it is at the initial hit—and you feel those Gs." At 100 feet the car is already traveling over 100 miles per hour.

Between the start and 150 feet off the line, the rear tires transition from their flattened state to one in which they are more rounded.

Above: Once the car has stopped following the burnout, the driver pushes in the clutch and engages the reverser. As the clutch is eased out, the car will back toward the starting line. The driver must rely on one of the crew members for guidance because there are no rearview mirrors on a Top Fuel dragster.

Once stopped at the starting line, the crew checks for leaks or any other situation that might cause a problem during the upcoming run. The crew chief makes a final adjustment to the barrel valve or removes an air bleed plug from the injector to set the idle. The stop that was added to the throttle for the burnout is also removed and is usually shown to the driver to demonstrate that it was, in fact, removed. During this time the driver's job is to keep the clutch pedal depressed, disengage the reverser, and hold the brake.

It's during this transition that tire shake can occur. When the tires shake, they lose traction. Tire shake occurs when the tire tread starts rolling over itself in the transition from wide and flat to tall and round. Tire shake is hard for spectators to see from the stands, but it can be felt on the ground when standing by the side of the track. Distinct chatter marks are left on the track where the tire slapped the racing surface. Extreme slow motion video used on today's television coverage clearly shows tire shake and what it does to a car. A driver will often "drive through" a mild tire shake, meaning that it corrects itself without any driver input. Severe tire shake results in the tires breaking loose. This is how Scelzi describes tire shake: "Put your head in a paint shaker, and that is probably as close to it as you can come. It's the most brutal, violent thing your body will ever experience." When drivers feel tire shake they will often "pedal" the car, which means they quickly let off and reapply the throttle. This is most noticeable to spectators when there is a momentary interruption in the steady stream of header flames. This slight adjustment is often enough to stop the shaking and to allow the tires to regain their grip on the track.

Pedaling a Top Fuel dragster is something that cannot be taught. Experienced drivers have turned it into an art form. It may be as simple as a momentary slap of the throttle. Or it may be a synchronized throttle-and-brake

Once the crew is finished checking the car, the driver, in this case drag racing legend Shirley Muldowney, is motioned ahead to the pre-stage lights. Because of the length of the car, one of the crew members stationed at the front of the car motions the driver ahead and signals to stop the car at a predetermined distance from the lights.

Only four-tenths of a second elapse between the time the Christmas tree flashes the yellow lights and the green light illuminates. A good reaction time means that the driver stabbed the throttle before he or she actually saw the green light.

ballet played out in thousandths of a second. When a Top Fuel dragster starts to smoke the tires or gets loose, it turns sideways. When a bite is reestablished, the cars have a tendency to tip over. "The toughest thing to learn in drag racing is patience," says Scelzi, "especially when your adrenaline meter is pegged and you're trying to get back on the gas as quick as you can."

In one of his first Top Fuel finals, Scelzi was on and off the throttle nine times. "I realized what I was doing wrong! I was still letting the car settle down, but I was violently back on the throttle." Scelzi learned that he needed to

smoothly reapply the throttle. He also learned that he needed to grab the brake to slow the tire speed. "When it smokes the tire, the tire goes instantly to 320 miles an hour, it's like being in water. So I've learned to grab the brake and roll the throttle down with the brake on and then release the brake. If it doesn't come back, start over."

Pedaling may sound simple from the vantage point of one's favorite easy chair; but it's much more difficult to execute this sequence in a few fractions of a second when you're sitting in front of a 6,000-horsepower, fire-breathing engine. "One of my most memorable races

As the engine's torque reaches the tires, they flatten out and grab as much of the track as possible. This car has dropped so low that its air deflectors in front of the headers are touching the racing surface.

As the car moves away from the starting line, the rear tires start to unwrap. It's during this transition that tire shake occurs.

Often when a Top Fuel dragster leaves the line, the front tires are inches off the ground for 1 or 2 seconds into the run. For this reason, it's important for the car to be pointing down the center of the lane when it's staged.

was last year," recalls Scelzi. "I was racing Mike Dunn. We both smoked the tires at the same time and I recovered. It went another 400 feet and smoked the tires again and I did it again. I ran 4.97, which was the absolute best job of peddling I'd ever done. I was so thrilled and so excited about it because I controlled it."

If the tires don't shake and if the car hooks up properly, the driver is in for a great ride. The engine will maintain 8,200 rpm for at least 1 second into the run. At that point the clutch timers start feeding in more clutch. As the clutch comes in, the load on the engine

increases, dropping the engine rpm to approximately 6,000. It's at this point that the maximum load is on the engine, and additional fuel must be added. By midtrack, approximately 3 seconds into the run, the clutch is "one-to-one." This means that the clutch is no longer slipping and the engine and driveshaft speed are the same. Once the clutch is one-to-one and the engine is coming back up to full rpm, the fuel mixture is leaned out, because the engine is no longer under the tremendous load. In 3.2 seconds the car is at midtrack and will be clocking over 270 miles per hour. On the last half of the track, only an additional 50 to 70 miles per hour will be gained because of aerodynamic drag. Whistling through the traps at 320 miles per hour equates to approximately 8,400 rpm.

Inside the car, the driver hears a slightly different noise than what the fans hear in the stands. "You can hear some of the valve train, some of the blower belt and gear drive noise because the exhaust is pointing behind you; you're ahead of the exhaust noise," says Dixon. Dropping a cylinder during a run is an instant loss of 750 horsepower. "If it puts out a cylinder, you can hear the engine change pitch and tone—you can really pick it up," Scelzi says. "You hear it all. Yesterday I dropped a cylinder at about the 1,000-foot mark and it sounded like the motor went under water. It wasn't singing like it was before."

Top Fuel drivers can also recognize when the car is on a good run. "A 320-mile-per-hour run is different than a 312," says Scelzi. "You can tell because the power is good from the beginning all the way to the finish line. A lot of times on a run with good e.t., it will quit at 1,100 feet." To "quit" means the engine's power curve has flattened out. While the car may run a respectable elapsed time, the speed will noticeably fall off. "I ran a 4.64 elapsed time and shut off before 1,200 feet," recalls Scelzi. "I was surprised it ran 303 miles per hour; I thought it ran 290. It was running so well early, that shutting it off didn't hurt the e.t. that much, but it hurt the speed a lot."

A fraction of a second before the car hits the finish line, the driver reaches over to release the parachutes. "When the parachute comes out, that's the best feeling in the world, because you know that you're somewhat under control," says Kenny Bernstein, driver of the *Budweiser King* dragster. "After the parachute's out, I pull the fuel shutoff. The motor is still makin' noise and it finally gears down and dies as you're starting to turn the corner. It's the most serene time of the run. It's very quiet. All you hear is the motor crackling."

At the hit of the throttle, the driver of a Top Fuel dragster experiences approximately 3.5 Gs. Within 2 to 3 seconds, the G-force is up to 5 as the clutch starts to lock up.

Top Fuel dragsters are required to have two parachutes. Often the driver may open only one after a run to assist in slowing the car. ©*Joe Veraldi*

Doug Herbert, driver of the *Snap On Tools* Top Fuel dragster, describes it this way: "Probably one of the best parts is when you get the car stopped and you climb out at the other end. That's when it's all done. There are so many things going on in your mind when you're going down the track. I really don't know if it's a lot of fun. I think it's a lot of excitement. It's definitely fun when you get out of the car, and you just beat Scelzi or you just beat Kenny [Bernstein]."

Top Fuel drivers will tell you that there are a lot of ways to lose in drag racing. You can't make up for a mistake on the next lap. There are no next laps. If everything goes well, a Top Fuel driver will drive a total of 1 mile in competition on race day. Hours of preparation are funneled down to a single 4.5-second run. There is no margin for error in that 4.5 seconds. "There aren't words in the English language to describe what it's like," says Scelzi. "It's the baddest ride you've ever been on. It's the most horrific, and it's the most outstanding sense of accomplishment, fear, and everything rolled into one that you could ever put in 4.5 seconds." Larry Dixon says, "I wish we raced on half-mile tracks instead of quarter-mile, so I could enjoy the feeling more. It's like the drug that keeps you coming back, because its only 4.5 seconds long."

Index

American Drag Racing
ISBN:0-7603-0871-3

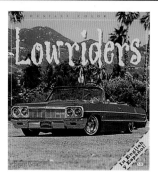

Lowriders
ISBN: 0-7603-0962-0

The American Car Dealership
ISBN: 0-7603-0639-7

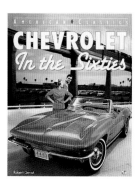

Chevrolet in the Sixties
ISBN:0-7603-0209-X

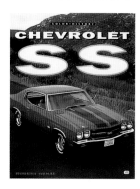

Chevrolet SS
ISBN: 0-7603-0715-6

Vintage & Historic Drag Racers
ISBN: 0-7603-0435-1

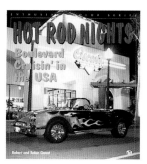

Hot Rod Nights:
Boulevard Crusin' in the USA
ISBN: 0-7603-0288-X

Retro Rods
ISBN: 0-7603-0919-1

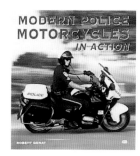

Modern Police Motorcycles in Action
ISBN: 0-7603-0522-6